Rice Cooker Cookbook:

Healthy and Easy Rice Cooker Recipes for Smart People on a Budget!

Henry Wilson

Copyright © [Henry Wilson]

All rights reserved. No part of this guide may be reproduced in any form without permission in writing from the publisher except in the case of brief quotations embodied in critical articles or reviews.

CONTENTS

INTRODUCTION 7

WHY USE A RICE COOKER 8

1. POULTRY RECIPES 9
   - GARLIC BUTTER CHICKEN 9
   - SHREDDED CHICKEN TACO MEAT 9
   - SHREDDED CHICKEN 10
   - BUTTER CHICKEN 11
   - FALL-OFF-THE-BONE CHICKEN 13
   - PAPRIKA CHICKEN 14
   - WHITE CHICKEN CHILI 15
   - CHICKEN CURRY 16
   - GREEN CHILE CHICKEN 17
   - CHILE VERDE 18

2. MEAT RECIPES 20
   - BEEF CURRY STEW 20
   - BEEF SHORT RIBS 21
   - MEXICAN BEEF 22
   - POT ROAST & GRAVY 23
   - CARNITAS LETTUCE WRAPS 24
   - JAMAICAN JERK PORK ROAST 26
   - PORK AND KRAUT 27
   - PORK CHOPS 28
   - PORK BELLY & SPICED RICE 29
   - CARNE ASADA (MEXICAN BRAISED BEEF) 30

3. FISH AND SEAFOOD RECIPES 32
   - SPICY BRAZILIAN FISH STEW 32
   - STEAMED WILD-CAUGHT CRAB LEGS 33
   - INDIAN FISH CURRY 34
   - STEAMED SHRIMP AND ASPARAGUS 36
   - FISH SAAG 37
   - LEMON GARLIC SALMON 39
   - LOBSTER TAILS WITH BUTTER SAUCE 40
   - CREAMY SHRIMP SCAMPI 42
   - SALMON WITH CHILI-LIME SAUCE 43

SEAFOOD GUMBO 44

4. RICE RECIPES 47

RICE COOKER PARMESAN RICE RECIPE 47
ARTICHOKE MIXED WITH BROWN RICE 48
ASPARAGUS RICE WITH SEARED SCALLOPS 49
AVOCADO BOWL WITH YOGURT SAUCE 51
BAKED RICE CASSEROLE WITH ARTICHOKES AND MUSHROOMS 52
KOREAN RICE BOWL 54
WILD RICE AND CHICKEN LIVER CROSTINI 56
SEAWEED MIXED RICE 57
TROPICAL LONG GRAIN SALAD 58
TERIYAKI RICE BURGER 60

5. APPETIZERS AND SIDE DISHES 63

TUNA & AVOCADO PLATE 63
THAI GREEN CHICKEN CURRY 64
TEMPURA BOWL 66
TEMARI SUSHI 67
SHRIMP STIR-FRIED RICE 69
SHIITAKE MUSHROOM RICE 71
SALSA VERDE STYLE BROWN RICE 72
SALMON TERIYAKI WITH MIXED VEGETABLES OVER RICE 74
RICE SPRINKLES ONIGIRI 76
RICE OMELET 77

6. DAIRY RECIPES 80

CHICKEN BACON CHOWDER 80
CHICKEN CORDON BLEU SOUP 81
MEXICAN CHICKEN SOUP 82
GARLIC BUTTER CHICKEN WITH CREAM CHEESE SAUCE 83
CHICKEN TIKKA MASALA 84
BUFFALO CHICKEN MEATBALLS 86
COCONUT CHICKEN 87
CAULIFLOWER MASHED POTATOES 88
CHUNKY CHILI 89
GHEE RICE 91

7. SOUPS AND STEWS 93

TACO SOUP 93
BEEF MINESTRONE SOUP 94

MACARONI SOUP 95

RICE COOKER DHAL 96

CHICKEN & DAIKON SOUP 97

ULTIMATE SHRIMP SOUP 98

TOM YUM SOUP..99

CLEAR VEGETABLE BROTH SOUP 100

HAINANESE CHICKEN RICE 101

RICE COOKER MISO SOUP 102

8. NOODLES RECIPES 104

INSTANT NOODLES IN RICE COOKER 104

NOODLES AND VEGETABLES 105

EASY CHICKEN PASTA NOODLES 106

BRAISED HAKUSAI CHINESE CABBAGE WITH DRIED SCALLOPS & SHIRATAKI 107

RICE COOKER SPAGHETTI WITH MEATBALLS 108

CREAMY RICE COOKER MACARONI 109

YUM PASTA NOODLES 110

RICE NOODLES WITH BEEF 111

EASY SPAGHETTI IN A RICE COOKER 112

RICE COOKER NOODLES WITH MUSHROOMS AND CORN 113

9. VEGETABLE AND EGG RECIPES 116

VEGETABLE BIRYANI 116

VEGETABLE CURRY RICE 117

VEGETABLE PILAF 118

RICE COOKER FIESTA MEXICAN RICE 120

PERFECT HARD BOILED EGGS 121

RICE COOKER SAAG 122

SAVOY CABBAGE WITH CREAM SAUCE 123

ARTICHOKES WITH LEMON TARRAGON DIPPING SAUCE 125

BRUSSELS SPROUTS 126

GREEN BEANS WITH BACON 127

10. DESSERTS 129

PUMPKIN PIE PUDDING 129

MOLTEN BROWNIE CUPS 130

KETO GLUTEN-FREE COCONUT ALMOND CAKE 131

KETO CARROT CAKE 133

CHEESECAKE 134

KETO CREME BRULEE 136

THE ULTIMATE RICE COOKER CAKE 137

Apple Rice Cooker Cake 138
Rice Cooker Upside-Down Pineapple Cake 140
Rice Cooker Lemon Cake 141

CONCLUSION 143

Introduction

If you love one-pot, easy meals that can put dinner on the table with the push of a button this cookbook is for you. You'll learn how to cook rice and meat at the same time, so your cooking time is cut in half. Prepare healthy dishes and meals for your family with the power of steam.

All of the recipes are for meals you would usually make at home without using a rice cooker. It is our guarantee that making them becomes much easier when you are using a rice cooker. So, all you have to do is read on until the end of this book and you can get started with cooking in a rice cooker.

WHY USE A RICE COOKER

Have you tried the rice cooker yet? This multicooker makes it easy to cook recipes that taste as though you had spent all day cooking them — perfect for busy people that want real food with minimal prep. These rice cooker recipes take advantage of all the amazing functions this all-in-one appliance offers.

One key way to make your diet easier? Meal prepping. One time-saving kitchen gadget to make meal prepping easier? The rice cooker. You probably know where we're going with this. Check out these 100 meals you can make in the rice cooker so that you've got time to live your best healthy life.

1. POULTRY RECIPES

GARLIC BUTTER CHICKEN

Preparation Time: 40 Minutes

Yield: 4 Servings

Ingredients

- 4 chicken breasts, whole or chopped
- ¼ cup turmeric ghee (or use regular ghee with 1 teaspoon turmeric powder)
- 1 teaspoon salt (add more to taste)
- 10 cloves garlic, peeled and diced

Directions

1. Add the chicken breasts to the cooker pot.
2. Add the ghee, (turmeric), salt, and diced garlic to the pressure cooker pot.
3. Set cooker on high for 35 minutes. Follow your cooker's instructions for releasing the pressure.
4. Shred the chicken breast in the pot.
5. Serve with additional ghee if needed.

Nutritional Information

- Calories: 404
- Fat: 21g
- Carbs: 3g
- Protein: 45g

SHREDDED CHICKEN TACO MEAT

Preparation Time: 50 Minutes

Yield: 4 Servings

Ingredients

- 4 chicken breasts
- 4 bell peppers, sliced
- 1 onion, sliced
- 2 Tablespoons paprika
- 2 Tablespoons garlic powder
- 1 Tablespoon cumin powder
- 1 teaspoon chili powder
- 3 Tablespoons ghee or coconut oil
- 2 Tablespoons salt or to taste
- ½ teaspoon black pepper

Directions

1. Place all the ingredients (chicken, bell peppers, onion, seasoning, oil) into the cooker pot and mix the ingredients together well.
2. Set cooker to cook on high pressure for 25 minutes.
3. Follow your cooker's instructions on releasing pressure from the cooker.
4. Shred the chicken breast meat and add extra seasoning to taste.
5. Serve with lettuce or kale leaves or by itself with some guacamole.

Nutritional Information

- Calories: 230
- Fat: 12g
- Carbs: 12g
- Protein: 19g

SHREDDED CHICKEN

Preparation Time: 20 Minutes

Yield: 4 Servings

Ingredients

- 4 pounds chicken breast
- ½ cup water or chicken broth
- 1 teaspoon salt
- ½ teaspoon black pepper

Directions

1. Add all of the ingredients to the Pot.
2. Secure the lid, close the valve and cook for 20 minutes at high pressure.
3. Quick release pressure.
4. Shred the chicken with two forks.
5. Store the chicken in an air-tight container with the liquid to help keep the meat moist.

Nutritional Information

- Calories: 225
- Fat: 9g
- Carbs: 0g
- Protein: 30g

BUTTER CHICKEN

Preparation Time: 20 Minutes

Yield: 4 Servings

Ingredients

- 2 tablespoons ghee
- 1 onion, diced
- 5 teaspoons minced garlic
- 1 teaspoon minced ginger

- 1 ½ pounds skinless and boneless chicken thighs, cut into quarters
- Spices
- 1 teaspoon coriander powder
- 1 teaspoon garam masala
- 1 teaspoon paprika
- 1 teaspoon salt
- 1 teaspoon turmeric
- ¼ teaspoon black pepper
- ¼ teaspoon cayenne
- ¼ teaspoon ground cumin
- 1 (15 ounce) can tomato sauce
- Add later:
- 2 green bell peppers, chopped into medium sized chunks/squares
- ½ cup heavy cream or full-fat coconut milk
- Pinch of dried fenugreek leaves (kasoori methi)
- Cilantro, garnish

Directions

1. Press the sauté button and add the ghee and onions to the pot. Stir-fry the onions for 6-7 minutes or until the onions begin to brown.
2. Add the garlic, ginger and chicken. Stir-fry the chicken for 6-7 minutes or until the outside of the chicken is no longer pink.
3. Add the spices and give everything a good mix.
4. Stir in the tomato sauce.
5. Secure the lid, close the valve and cook for 8 minutes at high pressure.
6. Open the valve to quick release any remaining pressure.
7. Press the sauté button, add the bell peppers and cook until they soften to your liking.
8. Stir in the cream and fenugreek leaves.

9. Garnish with cilantro if desired, then serve.

Nutritional Information

- Calories: 243
- Fat: 15g
- Carbs: 14g
- Protein: 12g

FALL-OFF-THE-BONE CHICKEN

Preparation Time: 30 Minutes

Yield: 4 Servings

Ingredients

- 1 whole - 4lb. organic chicken
- 1 Tbsp. Organic Virgin Coconut Oil
- 1 tsp. paprika
- 1½ cups Pacific Organic Bone Broth (Chicken)
- 1 tsp. dried thyme
- ¼ tsp. freshly ground black pepper
- 2 Tbsp. lemon juice
- ½ tsp. sea salt
- 6 cloves garlic, peeled

Directions

1. In a small bowl, combine paprika, thyme, salt, and pepper. Rub seasoning over outside of bird.
2. Heat oil in the cooker to shimmering. Add chicken, breast side down and cook 6-7 minutes.
3. Flip the chicken and add broth, lemon juice and garlic cloves.
4. Lock cooker lid and set for 25 minutes on high.
5. Let the cooker release naturally.

6. Remove from cooker and let stand for 5 minutes before carving.

Nutritional Information

- Calories: 243
- Fat: 15g
- Carbs: 14g
- Protein: 12g

PAPRIKA CHICKEN

Preparation Time: 30 Minutes

Yield: 4 Servings

Ingredients

- 1 free range whole chicken
- 1 tbsp olive oil
- 1 tbsp dried paprika
- 1 tbsp curry powder
- 1 tsp dried turmeric
- 1 tsp salt

Directions

1. Mix the spices, oil and salt in a small cup.
2. Oil the inside of the cooker, place the whole chicken inside.
3. Pat the chicken dry with kitchen paper. This allows the spice mixture to stick to the chicken.
4. Spoon the spice mixture all over the whole chicken.
5. Turn the cooker on and cook on HIGH for 30 minutes.
6. Always test the chicken at its thickest part to confirm it is thoroughly cooked. I push a skewer into the breast and drumstick, to make sure the liquid that drains off is clear.

Nutritional Information

- Calories: 270
- Fat: 9g
- Carbs: 5g
- Protein: 33g

WHITE CHICKEN CHILI

Preparation Time: 20 Minutes

Yield: 4 Servings

Ingredients

- 2 pounds of boneless, skinless chicken breasts
- 2 onions, diced
- 4 stalks celery, diced
- 1-2 jalapeño pepper, minced – adjust according to taste
- 10 cloves garlic, minced
- 1 tablespoon chili powder
- 1 tablespoon salt, adjust to taste
- 1 teaspoon cumin
- 1 teaspoon coriander powder
- 1 teaspoon oregano
- ½ teaspoon freshly crushed black pepper, adjust to taste
- 4 cups chicken broth
- 1 (1 pound) bag of corn frozen, rinsed (optional if paleo)
- 1 (15 ounce) can cannellini beans, rinsed (optional if paleo)
- Serve with cilantro, hot sauce, cheese if desired

Directions

1. Add all of the ingredients except for the cannellini beans and corn to the Pot.
2. Secure the lid, close the pressure valve and cook for 15 minutes at high pressure.

3. Open the valve to quick release any pressure (this will allow the steam to escape and you'll be able to open the lid sooner than waiting for natural release).
4. Shred the chicken in the pot then add the cannellini beans and corn to the pot. Press the sauté button and cook for 5 minutes or until the beans and corn are heated through.

Nutritional Information

- Calories: 481
- Fat: 30g
- Carbs: 5g
- Protein: 39g

CHICKEN CURRY

Preparation Time: 30 Minutes

Yield: 4 Servings

Ingredients

- 1 ½ pounds chicken drumsticks (approx. 5 drumsticks), skin removed
- 1 (13.5 ounce) can Organic Coconut Milk
- 1 onion, finely chopped
- 4 cloves garlic, minced (I used my garlic press)
- 1-inch knob fresh ginger, minced
- 1 Serrano pepper, minced
- 1 tablespoon Garam Masala
- ½ teaspoon cayenne
- ½ teaspoon paprika
- ½ teaspoon turmeric
- salt and pepper, adjust to taste

Directions

1. Cut around the bottom of each drumstick to cut the tendons – then use a paper towel to remove the skin from the chicken.
2. Add the chicken and the rest of the ingredients to a cooker and cook for 30 minutes.
3. Watch as the tender meat barely clings to the bones… then eat

Nutritional Information

- Calories: 347
- Fat: 21g
- Carbs: 8g
- Protein: 30g

GREEN CHILE CHICKEN

Preparation Time: 40 Minutes

Yield: 4 Servings

Ingredients

- 3 pounds Boneless Skinless Chicken Thighs, fresh or thawed
- 4 ounces Green Chiles (1 can)
- 2 teaspoons Garlic Salt
- ½ cup White Onions, diced (optional for some extra flavor)

Directions

1. Cook chicken in a pot for 20 minutes.
2. After that, drain juices from the pot
3. Mix together green chiles and garlic salt (and optional onions).
4. Pour mixture over chicken, and cook for 200 more minutes.
5. Remove chicken from pot, and shred with a fork.

6. Serve with all the assorted side dishes that normally accompany tacos, or wrapped up in burritos. YUM!

Nutritional Information

- Calories: 390
- Fat: 18g
- Carbs: 6g
- Protein: 40g

CHILE VERDE

Preparation Time: 1 Hour 20 Minutes

Yield: 4 Servings

Ingredients

- 2 lbs boneless, chopped, pork stewing meat, or chicken.
- 3 Tbsp butter or oil of choice for paleo.
- 3 tbsp cilantro, chopped fine.
- 1½ cups salsa verde
- 5 cloves garlic, minced.
- ¼ tsp sea salt.
- 1 tbsp extra cilantro for garnish.

Directions

1. Put the cooker pot on high and put two tbsps of the butter into pot and let melt.
2. Add 4 of the minced garlic cloves and 2 tbsps cilantro to the cooker and stir.
3. Heat a large fry pan to medium high on stove top, and melt 1 tbsp butter in it.
4. Add one tbsp mince garlic and 1 tbsp minced cilantro.
5. Add cubed pork meat to fry pan and brown sears all side of pork until just browned not cooked through.
6. Add pork meat and garlic cilantro butter to the pot.

7. Add 1½ cups salsa verde to the pot and stir around.
8. Cover the cooker and cook on high for 60 minutes
9. Serve in lettuce cups, or tortillas, or over cauliflower rice.

Nutritional Information

- Calories: 206
- Fat: 8g
- Carbs: 2g
- Protein: 29g

2. Meat Recipes

Beef Curry Stew

Preparation Time: 50 Minutes

Yield: 4 Servings

Ingredients

- 2.5 lb beef stew chunks (or buy a roast and chop into small cubes)
- 1 lb broccoli florets
- 3 zucchinis, chopped
- ½ cup chicken broth (or use water)
- 2 Tablespoons curry powder
- 1 Tablespoon garlic power
- Salt to taste
- 14 oz can coconut milk

Directions

1. Add all the ingredients into the cooker pot.
2. Mix well and try to keep the beef on the bottom of the pot.
3. Set on high pressure (use the manual setting on the Pot) for 45 minutes.
4. Check your cooker's instructions for releasing pressure.
5. Gently stir in the coconut milk and add any additional salt to taste
6. Serve in bowls.

Nutritional Information

- Calories: 490
- Fat: 30g
- Carbs: 8g

- Protein: 40g

BEEF SHORT RIBS

Preparation Time: 60 Minutes

Yield: 4 Servings

Ingredients

- 2 lb boneless beef short ribs (or 4 lb bone-in beef short ribs)
- 1 onion, diced
- 2 Tablespoons curry powder (optional)
- 6 star anise (optional)
- 1 Tablespoon Szechuan peppercorns (optional)
- 1 cup water
- 3 Tablespoons of tamari sauce
- 2 Tablespoons vodka (or white wine)
- 1 Tablespoon salt

Directions

1. Place all the ingredients into the rice cooker.
2. Press the Meat/Stew button and then set the timer for 45 minutes. (The cooker takes a few minutes of prep to get ready and then a few minutes to bring the pressure down, so the total cook time is closer to 1 hour.)

Nutritional Information

- Calories: 490
- Fat: 30g
- Carbs: 8g
- Protein: 40g

Mexican Beef

Preparation Time: 45 Minutes

Yield: 4 Servings

Ingredients

- 2½ pounds boneless beef short ribs, beef brisket, or beef chuck roast cut into 1½- to 2-inch cubes
- 1 tablespoon chili powder
- 1½ teaspoons kosher salt (Diamond Crystal brand)
- 1 tablespoon ghee or fat of choice
- 1 medium onion, thinly sliced
- 1 tablespoon tomato paste
- 6 garlic cloves, peeled and smashed
- ½ cup roasted tomato salsa
- ½ cup bone broth
- ½ teaspoon Red Boat Fish Sauce
- freshly ground black pepper
- ½ cup minced cilantro (optional)
- 2 radishes, thinly sliced (optional)

Directions

1. In a large bowl, combine cubed beef, chili powder, and salt.
2. Press the "Sauté" button on your Pot and add the ghee to the cooker. Once the fat's melted, add the onions and sauté until translucent.
3. Stir in the tomato paste and garlic, and cook for 30 seconds or until fragrant.
4. Toss in the seasoned beef, and pour in the salsa, stock, and fish sauce.
5. Cover and lock the lid, and press the "Keep Warm/Cancel" button on the Pot. Press the "Manual" or "Pressure Cook" button to switch to the pressure cooking mode and cook for 35 minutes under high pressure.

6. When the stew is finished cooking, remove the pot from the heat and let the pressure release naturally.
7. Unlock the lid and season to taste with salt and pepper. At this point, you can plate and serve—or store the beef in the fridge for up to 4 days and reheat right before serving.
8. When you're ready to eat, top the hot stew with cilantro and radishes.

Nutritional Information

- Calories: 209
- Fat: 13g
- Carbs: 6g
- Protein: 18g

POT ROAST & GRAVY

Preparation Time: 20 Minutes

Yield: 4 Servings

Ingredients

- 4 pounds chuck roast, cut into 4 pieces
- a good pinch of salt
- freshly ground black pepper
- 1 1/2 cups beef broth
- 2 tablespoons balsamic vinegar
- 2 teaspoons fish sauce (optional, add more salt if omitting)
- 1 three inch sprig rosemary
- 4 three inch sprigs thyme
- 2 parsnips, peeled
- 4 carrots, peeled or scrubbed
- 6 cloves garlic, peeled
- chopped parsley and/or chives for serving, optional

Directions

1. Season the beef with salt and pepper and place in the cooker.
2. Place all of the remaining ingredients in the cooker. Lock on the lid and set it for 60 minutes on high pressure.
3. After the 60 minutes are up, allow the pressure to release naturally for 15 minutes.
4. Remove the meat to a plate, and the veggies to a blender.
5. Discard the rosemary and thyme stems. Pour the cooking liquid into a large jar or measuring cup. Once the fat rises to the top (this will happen quickly), remove and discard it with a large spoon or small ladle. Pour the remaining liquid into the blender with the vegetables and blend until smooth. Season to taste with salt and pepper. (you may or not need any, depending on the seasoning of the broth you used)
6. Roughly shred the meat using two forks. You can either stir some of the gravy into the meat or just pour it on top. Or both!
7. Serve with your favorite roasted or mashed potatoes, cauliflower mash, or any root vegetables, mashed or roasted.

Nutritional Information

Calories: 210

Fat: 16g

Carbs: 1g

Protein: 15g

CARNITAS LETTUCE WRAPS

Preparation Time: 50 Minutes

Yield: 4 Servings

Ingredients

- 1 tablespoon unsweetened cocoa powder
- 2 teaspoons sea salt
- 1 teaspoon cayenne pepper
- 2 teaspoons dried oregano
- 1 teaspoon white pepper
- 1 teaspoon garlic powder
- 1 teaspoon onion salt
- 1 teaspoon ground cumin
- 1/2 teaspoon ground coriander
- 1 (3-pound) pork shoulder or butt
- 2 tablespoons olive oil
- 2–3 cups water
- 1 head butter lettuce, washed and dried
- 1 small jalapeño, sliced
- 1/4 cup julienned radishes
- 1 medium avocado, diced
- 2 small Roma tomatoes, diced
- 2 limes, cut into wedges

Directions

1. In a small bowl, combine cocoa powder, salt, cayenne pepper, oregano, white pepper, garlic powder, onion salt, cumin, and coriander. Massage seasoning into pork shoulder and refrigerate covered overnight.
2. Press the Sauté button on the Pot. Add 2 tablespoons oil. Sear roast on all sides ensuring all sides are browned, about 8–10 minutes. Add enough water (2–3 cups) to almost cover the meat. Lock lid.
3. Press the Manual button and adjust time to 45 minutes. When the timer beeps, let pressure release naturally for 10 minutes. Quick-release any additional pressure until the float valve drops and then unlock lid.

4. Transfer pork to a platter. Using two forks, shred the meat. Discard all but 1/2 cup of cooking liquid. Add meat back into the Pot. Press the Sauté button and stir-fry meat
5. for 4-5 minutes creating some crispy edges. Toss with additional liquid.
6. Enjoy!

Nutritional Information

- Calories: 175
- Fat: 5g
- Carbs: 10g
- Protein: 18g

JAMAICAN JERK PORK ROAST

Preparation Time: 50 Minutes

Yield: 4 Servings

Ingredients

- 4 lb pork shoulder
- 1/4 cup Jamaican Jerk spice blend
- 1 Tbsp olive oil
- 1/2 cup beef stock or broth

Directions

1. Rub the roast with olive oil and coat with Jamaican Jerk spice blend.
2. Set your Pot to Saute and brown the meat on all sides.
3. Add the beef broth.
4. Seal the top according to instructions and cook on Manual, high pressure, for 45 minutes.
5. Release pressure according to instructions, shred and serve.

Nutritional Information

- Calories: 473
- Fat: 25g
- Carbs: 9g
- Protein: 50g

PORK AND KRAUT

Preparation Time: 50 Minutes

Yield: 4 Servings

Ingredients

- 2 to 3 pounds of pork roast
- 2 tablespoons Coconut Oil or ghee, butter, lard, etc
- 2 large Onions sliced or chopped
- 3 cloves Garlic peeled & sliced
- 1 cup Water, filtered
- 4 to 6 cups sauerkraut divided
- 1 pound hot dogs nitrate free, grass fed beef (optional)
- 1/2 pound kielbasa nitrate free, grass fed beef (optional)

Directions

1. Liberally season your pork roast with sea salt and pepper, set aside
2. Heat a large skillet over high heat until smoking. Add coconut oil and brown your pork roast on all sides (including the edges).
3. Place your browned pork roast on a rack in your cooker. Add water, garlic and onions. Again, season liberally with sea salt and pepper.
4. Cook under pressure for 35 minutes (press the meat/stew button)
5. Allow to naturally depressurize.

6. Once your cooker is depressurized, add in roughly 1/2 of your sauerkraut (we reserve 1/2 of it so that when we eat we can serve some raw to get the beneficial fermented bacteria)
7. Cook your pork & kraut under pressure for roughly 5 minutes.
8. Add hot dogs and kielbasa, cook under pressure for another 5 minutes. (no longer, or your hot dogs will break apart, trust me)
9. Allow to rest/cool slightly while you finish your mashed potatoes. Serve with both cooked and the reserved raw sauerkraut. Enjoy

Nutritional Information

- Calories: 336
- Fat: 11g
- Carbs: 6g
- Protein: 50g

PORK CHOPS

Preparation Time: 20 Minutes

Yield: 4 Servings

Ingredients

- 4 pork chops (boneless or bone in)
- 2 tbs coconut oil, divided
- 1 cup chicken broth
- one onion sliced
- 8 oz of mushrooms, chopped
- salt & pepper to taste
- 2 tbs butter or ghee

Directions

1. Heat up the cooker on high heat.
2. Salt and pepper both sides of the pork chops.
3. Once pot is hot, add in 1 tbs of coconut oil.
4. Add in pork chops to sear, do not crowd the pan you want a nice sear on each pork chop. I did mine in 2 batches. Sear on each side approximately 2 minutes. Remove chops and set aside.
5. Add remaining 1 tbs coconut oil to pot. Add in onions and saute for 2 minutes. Add in mushrooms and saute for another 2 minutes. Pour in chicken broth and scrape off any brown bits that are still remaining on the bottom of the pot.
6. Add pork chops back in with any liquid.
7. Turn heat down to main pressure and cook for 10 minutes.
8. Remove chops and cover to keep warm. Put the pot back on high heat to reduce the sauce down.
9. After the sauce rapidly boils for about 5 minutes, add in butter or ghee and remove from heat.
10. Serve chops with mushroom sauce on top.

Nutritional Information

- Calories: 328
- Fat: 17g
- Carbs: 1g
- Protein: 40g

PORK BELLY & SPICED RICE

Preparation Time: 20 Minutes

Yield: 4 Servings

Ingredients

- 1 pound pork belly, cooked and cubed
- 4 cups riced cauliflower

- 1/2 cup bone broth
- 1/2 red onion, sliced
- 1/2 cup cilantro, divided
- 2 green onions, sliced
- 1 tablespoon lime juice
- 3 cloves garlic, sliced
- 1 tablespoon animal fat
- 1 teaspoon turmeric
- 1 tablespoon oregano
- 1 tablespoon cumin
- 1/2 teaspoon salt

Directions

1. Place all ingredients, except 1/4 cup cilantro, in your Pot.
2. Place lid on the Pot.
3. Press Manual button.
4. Set time to 15 minutes.
5. Once dish is done cooking, turn off the cooker.
6. Allow pressure to release naturally for 10 minutes before opening lid.

Nutritional Information

- Calories: 328
- Fat: 17g
- Carbs: 1g
- Protein: 40g

CARNE ASADA (MEXICAN BRAISED BEEF)

Preparation Time: 20 Minutes

Yield: 4 Servings

Ingredients

- 3 pounds beef stew meat grass fed/pastured
- 3 tablespoons Salt
- 1 tablespoon organic chili powder
- 1 tablespoon organic cumin
- 1 pinch Crushed Red Pepper Flakes
- 2+ tablespoons Olive Oil
- 1/2 medium lime, juiced
- 1 cup bone broth
- 3 ounces tomato paste roughly 1/2 of a 6 ounce can
- 1 large Onion

Directions

1. Trim beef stew pieces as they need to be bite sized.
2. Toss beef stew pieces with dry seasonings.
3. Working in batches, over medium/high heat brown seasoned beef pieces in olive oil in a dutch oven or heavy bottomed pot.
4. Combine browned beef pieces with the remaining ingredients and mix well.
5. Cook under high/standard pressure for 35 minutes. Can be quickly depressurized or allowed to depressurize naturally.

Nutritional Information

- Calories: 287
- Fat: 14g
- Carbs: 6g
- Protein: 30g

3. Fish and Seafood Recipes

Spicy Brazilian Fish Stew

Preparation Time: 20 Minutes

Yield: 4 Servings

Ingredients

- 1 pound wild caught cod or other wild caught white fish
- 1 medium lime, juiced
- 1 medium jalapeno pepper (seeds removed)
- 1 medium Onion
- 1 medium red pepper
- 1 medium yellow pepper
- 2 cloves Garlic
- 1 teaspoon Paprika
- 2 cups Chicken Bone Broth
- 2 cups chopped tomatoes
- 1+ teaspoons Sea Salt
- 1/4 teaspoon Black Pepper
- 15 ounces coconut milk (canned)
- Optional garnishes
- chopped fresh cilantro
- additional lime wedges

Directions

1. Place the fish in a large nonreactive mixing bowl, add the lime juice, and set aside to marinate while you proceed with the recipe.
2. Heat up your cooker, and add the olive oil. Once it is hot, add the peppers and onions saute, stirring often, until the

onions are translucent, 3 to 4 minutes. Add the garlic and saute for 30 seconds.
3. Add the spices, tomatoes and broth, stir well to incorporate. Bring the mixture to a boil.
4. Then add the fish (with the lime juice) and the coconut milk. Stir to combine, and bring the liquid to a boil. Cover the cooker, reduce the heat to medium-low, and cook until the flesh of the fish starts to flake, about 10 minutes.
5. Remove the cover, sprinkle the cilantro over the fish, and serve accompanied by wedges of lime.

Nutritional Information

- Calories: 360
- Fat: 22g
- Carbs: 13g
- Protein: 12g

STEAMED WILD-CAUGHT CRAB LEGS

Preparation Time: 10 Minutes

Yield: 4 Servings

Ingredients

- 2 pounds of wild-caught Snow Crab legs
- 1 cup of water
- 1/3 cup of salted grass-fed butter, melted (or ghee)
- lemon slices

Directions

1. Place the metal trivet in the bottom of your cooker.
2. Add 1 cup water.
3. Add the crab legs to the pot. If it helps to thaw them slightly so you can fit them all in the cooker, that's fine.
4. Place the lid on the cooker and seal the vent.

5. Press the "Manual" button and adjust the time to 3 minutes.
6. Quick release the pressure as soon as the cooker beeps.
7. Use tongs to carefully transfer the cooked crab legs to a platter for serving.
8. Serve with melted grass-fed butter and lemon slices!

Nutritional Information

- Calories: 100
- Fat: 2g
- Carbs: 0g
- Protein: 16g

INDIAN FISH CURRY

Preparation Time: 20 Minutes

Yield: 4 Servings

Ingredients

- 2 Tbsp coconut oil
- 10 curry leaves optional
- 1 cup onion chopped
- 1 Tbsp garlic
- 1 Tbsp ginger
- 1/2 serrano or jalapeno chili pepper sliced or slit (use 1 whole chili for spicy)
- 1 cup tomato chopped
- 1 tsp ground coriander
- 1/4 tsp ground cumin
- 1/2 tsp turmeric
- 1/2 tsp black pepper
- 1 tsp salt
- 2 Tbsp water for deglazing
- 1 cup canned coconut milk about 1/2 of 14 oz. can

- 1 1/2 lbs fish fillets e.g. firm fish like cod or haddock, cut into 2-inch pieces
- 1 tsp lime juice
- Fresh cilantro leaves for garnish optional
- Fresh tomato slices for garnish optional

Directions

1. Select the 'Saute' function and pre-heat the cooker.
2. Add coconut oil to the pre-heated inner pot of cooker and allow it to heat up.
3. Add curry leaves (if using) and stir for about 20 seconds.
4. Add onions, garlic, ginger and green chilies to the inner pot.
5. Stir onion mixture until onions are translucent.
6. Add tomatoes and saute until the tomatoes release their liquid and start breaking down.
7. Add in coriander, cumin, turmeric, black pepper, and salt.
8. Saute until spices are fragrant, about 30 seconds. Be careful not to burn!
9. Deglaze with a tablespoon or two of water.
10. Stir in coconut milk.
11. Carefully add in fish pieces.
12. Gently lift up the fish pieces so that the coconut milk reaches the floor of the inner pot, and the fish is coated with the sauce.
13. Close the lid and pressure cook for 2 minutes.
14. Do a Quick Release of pressure (QR) and open the lid.
15. Add lime juice to the cooker.
16. Gently stir the curry without breaking up the fish.
17. Carefully remove fish and gravy into a serving bowl. Garnish with chopped cilantro and fresh tomato slices.
1. Serve over rice.

Nutritional Information

- Calories: 307

- Fat: 15g
- Carbs: 6g
- Protein: 36g

STEAMED SHRIMP AND ASPARAGUS

Preparation Time: 20 Minutes

Yield: 4 Servings

Ingredients

- 1 pound peeled and deveined shrimp, frozen or fresh
- 1 bunch of asparagus
- 1 teaspoon olive oil
- ½ tablespoon Cajun seasoning (or your seasoning of choice – lemon juice with salt and pepper would be delicious too)

Directions

2. Add 1 cup of water to your cooker.
3. Insert the stainless steel steam rack that comes with your cooker to the bottom of the pot with the handles up (or silicone steamer).
4. Place the asparagus on the steam rack in a single layer (or silicone steamer) to act as a bed for your shrimp.
5. Place the shrimp on top of the asparagus.
6. Drizzle the olive oil over the shrimp and then season with the Cajun seasoning (or your seasoning of choice).
7. Cover and lock the lid.
8. Select "Steam" mode and press the "-" button until it reads 2 minutes and then select "Low Pressure" (the default is "High Pressure"). Also make sure to set the top knob to "Sealing" and not "Venting". I used frozen shrimp so you'll want to decrease the time to 1 minute for fresh shrimp.
9. The cooker will beep at you when it finishes cooking the shrimp.

10. To avoid over-cooking, move the top knob from "Sealing" to "Venting" to manually release the pressure. Once all of the pressure releases the steam will no longer come out of the vent and you'll be able to open the lid.

Nutritional Information

- Calories: 155
- Fat: 2g
- Carbs: 15g
- Protein: 22g

FISH SAAG

Preparation Time: 20 Minutes

Yield: 4 Servings

Ingredients

For the Sauce

- 1 cup chopped onion
- 1 cup chopped tomato
- 1/2 cup canned coconut milk out of a 14.5 ounce can of coconut milk
- 1 tablespoon minced ginger
- 1 tablespoon minced garlic
- 1 teaspoon garam masala
- 1 teaspoon tumeric
- 1/2-1 teaspoon cayenne pepper
- 1 teaspoon salt
- 2 cups frozen spinach
- 1/4 cup water

For the Fish

- 1 pound semi-frozen haddock fillets about 1/2 inch thin and cut into 3-4 inch even bite size pieces or any other firm white fish such as cod or tilapia
- 1 teaspoon turmeric
- 1 teaspoon salt

Directions

1. Set out the fish on the kitchen counter to defrost and proceed with the steps listed below. By the time you gather all the ingredients and get to to the fish, it should be somewhat defrosted and ready for you.
2. Blend together the onions, tomatoes, ginger, garlic, and 1/2 cup of coconut milk. Pour this sauce into the inner liner of the cooker.
3. Stir in the salt, cayenne, turmeric and garam masala. Use the 1/4 cup of water to wash out the blender jar and pour that last bit of goodness into the pot.
4. Add in the frozen spinach and stir. The spinach or greens are what makes this a saag.
5. Place a steamer rack on top of this sauce.
6. For the Fish: Rub the fish cubes with oil, salt, and turmeric. Place the fish on a sheet of aluminum foil and fold the sheet over on all sides to make a securely-wrapped package. Place this package on top of the steamer rack.
7. Cook for 5 Minutes high pressure.
8. Allow it to release pressure naturally for 5 mins and then release all remaining pressure.
9. Very carefully lift up the package of fish, open one side of it, and tilt it so that all the cooking liquids pour into the sauce below. Set the package of fish aside. (You are doing this so that you don't break up the fish as you proceed to the next step which asks you to mix the sauce well.)
10. Pour in the reserved canned coconut milk and stir well until it is well incorporated. Only once this is done will you carefully open the package of fish and tilt the pieces of fish

into the spinach saag. Serve with rice, or naan, cauliflower rice, or zoodles (zucchini noodles).

Nutritional Information

- Calories: 155
- Fat: 2g
- Carbs: 15g
- Protein: 22g

LEMON GARLIC SALMON

Preparation Time: 20 Minutes

Yield: 4 Servings

Ingredients

- 1 1/2 pounds frozen salmon filets
- 1/4 cup lemon juice
- 3/4 cup water
- A few springs of fresh dill, basil, parsley or a mix
- 1/4 teaspoon garlic powder or to taste (or 2 cloves garlic, minced)
- 1/4 teaspoon sea salt or to taste
- 1/8 teaspoon black pepper
- 1 lemon, sliced thinly
- 1 tablespoon avocado oil or melted coconut oil

Directions

1. Pour water and lemon juice into your cooker. Add fresh herbs to the water/lemon juice mixture and place steamer rack in cooker.
2. Drizzle salmon with oil and season with salt and pepper. Sprinkle garlic powder over the salmon and place on the salmon in a single layer on the steamer rack in the cooker. Note: If your salmon pieces are frozen together, run them

under water until they are able to be separated. Stacking salmon might make it too thick too cook all the way through.
3. Layer lemon slices on top of the salmon.
4. Place the lid on the cooker, lock in place and turn the valve to sealing. Then use the Manual setting to cook on high pressure for 7 minutes.
5. Once the time is up, switch the valve to venting to quick release the pressure.
6. Enjoy warm over a salad, with roasted vegetables or any other way that you can dream up!

Nutritional Information

- Calories: 201
- Fat: 7g
- Carbs: 2g
- Protein: 31g

LOBSTER TAILS WITH BUTTER SAUCE

Preparation Time: 20 Minutes

Yield: 4 Servings

Ingredients

- Frozen Lobster Tails
- 1 Cup of water
- 1 Tablespoon of your favorite Old Bay Seasoning
- Butter Sauce Ingredients
- 1 cup butter
- 1 teaspoon minced garlic
- 1/2 teaspoon salt
- 1/2 teaspoon pepper
- 2 teaspoons lemon juice
- 1 teaspoon dill weed or cilantro whichever you prefer

Directions

1. Start by prepping the lobster tails for steaming. Use kitchen shears and cut a line down the inside of each shell. (I made the mistake of not doing this my first time and the lobsters curl up making them hard to cut when they are hot)
2. Add one cup of water in the Cooker.
3. Add 1 tablespoon of Old Bay seasoning to the water in the rice Cooker.
4. Place the trivet in the bottom of the Cooker on top of the water mixture.
5. Place 4 lobster tails shell side down.
6. Next, place the steamer basket on top of the first 4 lobster tails and add the remaining tails on the top of that steamer basket.
7. Lock the cover and make sure the vent is set to seal.
8. Now press the manual button and use the plus or minus buttons to adjust the minutes to 4 minutes. (Note: I used 4 minutes because the lobster tails were frozen)
9. It's important to know that your pressure cooker will take a while to heat up with frozen ingredients in it. I want to say mine took about 10 to 15 minutes to heat up and get going.
10. The timer will switch to say "on" when it is heating up. Once it's heated, it will start to count down the minutes from 4 when it is steaming.
11. When the lobster tails are steaming in the Cooker, this is when I make the butter sauce.
12. To make the butter sauce, simply place a tablespoon of butter in a frying pan and cooking it for about 3 minutes until it turns brown. Add the remaining butter and a teaspoon of fresh minced garlic. Once it has completely melted add the remaining ingredients (lemon juice, pepper, and either cilantro or dill weed seasonings) to the

butter mixture. Mix all the ingredients together and set aside.
13. Once the pressure cooker beeps telling you the time is up, turn it off and do a quick release of the steam. Careful not to place your hands on top of the button because that is where the steam comes out and it will burn you.
14. Once the steam has completely released, then unlock the lid and remove the lobster tails using kitchen tongs.
15. Serve the lobster tails immediately with the butter sauce.

Nutritional Information

- Calories: 246
- Fat: 47g
- Carbs: 1g
- Protein: 25g

CREAMY SHRIMP SCAMPI

Preparation Time: 10 Minutes

Yield: 4 Servings

Ingredients

- 2 tablespoons butter
- 1 pound shrimp, frozen
- 4 cloves garlic, minced
- 1/4-1/2 teaspoons red pepper flakes
- 1/2 teaspoons paprika
- 2 cups Carbanada low carb pasta (uncooked)
- 1 cup water or chicken broth
- 1/2 cup half and half
- 1/2 cup parmesan cheese
- salt, to taste
- pepper, to taste

Directions

1. Melt the butter in the cooker.
2. Add in garlic and red pepper flakes and cook until the garlic is slightly browned 1-2 minutes.
3. Add the paprika and then the frozen shrimp, salt, pepper, and noodles.
4. Pour in the broth. If using broth, don't add salt above.
5. Cook under pressure for 2 minutes an use quick release.
6. Turn the pot to Saute, add in half and half and cheese, and stir until melted.

Nutritional Information

- Calories: 312
- Fat: 9g
- Carbs: 5g
- Protein: 25g

SALMON WITH CHILI-LIME SAUCE

Preparation Time: 10 Minutes

Yield: 4 Servings

Ingredients

- For steaming salmon:
- 2 salmon fillets 5 ounces each
- 1 cup water
- sea salt to taste
- freshly ground black pepper to taste
- For chili-lime sauce:
- 1 jalapeno seeds removed and diced
- 1 lime juiced
- 2 cloves garlic minced
- 1 tablespoon honey
- 1 tablespoon olive oil
- 1 tablespoon hot water

- 1 tablespoon chopped fresh parsley
- 1/2 teaspoon paprika
- 1/2 teaspoon cumin

Directions

1. Combine and mix all sauce ingredients in a bowl with a pourable lip. Set aside.
2. Add water to the cooker. Place salmon fillets on top of a steam rack inside the pot.
3. Season the top of the salmon fillets with salt and pepper to your liking.
4. Cover and lock the lid. Select the steam mode and adjust the cooking time to 5 minutes at high pressure.
5. When the cooker is finished, use the quick release handle to release steam pressure and to stop the cooking.
6. Open the lid and transfer the salmon to a serving plate. Drizzle with chili-lime sauce and serve.

Nutritional Information

- Calories: 400
- Fat: 25g
- Carbs: 10g
- Protein: 30g

SEAFOOD GUMBO

Preparation Time: 20 Minutes

Yield: 4 Servings

Ingredients

- 24 ounces sea bass filets patted dry and cut into 2" chunks
- 3 tablespoons ghee or avocado oil
- 3 tablespoons cajun seasoning or creole seasoning
- 2 yellow onions diced

- 2 bell peppers diced
- 4 celery ribs diced
- 28 ounces diced tomatoes
- 1/4 cup tomato paste
- 3 bay leaves
- 1 1/2 cups bone broth
- 2 pounds medium to large raw shrimp deveined
- sea salt to taste
- black pepper to taste

Directions

1. Season the barramundi with some salt and pepper, and make sure they are as evenly coated as possible. Sprinkle half of the Cajun seasoning onto the fish and give it a stir; make sure it is coated well and set aside.
2. Put the ghee in the cooker and push "Sauté". Wait until it reads "Hot" and add the barramundi chunks. Sauté for about 4 minutes, until it looks cooked on both sides. Use a slotted spoon to transfer the fish to a large plate.
3. Add the onions, pepper, celery and the rest of the Cajun seasoning to the pot and sauté for 2 minutes until fragrant. Push "Keep Warm/Cancel". Add the cooked fish, diced tomatoes, tomato paste, bay leaves and bone broth to the pot and give it a nice stir. Put the lid back on the pot and set it to "Sealing." Push "Manual" and set the time for just 5 minutes! The cooker will slowly build up to a high pressure point and once it reaches that point, the gumbo will cook for 5 minutes.
4. Once the 5 minutes have ended, push the "Keep warm/Cancel" button. Cautiously change the "Sealing" valve over to "Venting," which will manually release all of the pressure. Once the pressure has been released (this will take a couple of minutes), remove the lid and change the setting to "Sauté" again. Add the shrimp and cook for about 3-4 minutes, or until the shrimp have become

opaque. Add some more sea salt and black pepper, to taste. Serve hot and top off with some cauliflower rice and chives.

Nutritional Information

- Calories: 297
- Fat: 16g
- Carbs: 11g
- Protein: 27g

4. RICE RECIPES

RICE COOKER PARMESAN RICE RECIPE

Preparation Time: 20 Minutes

Yield: 4 Servings

Ingredients

- 3 Tbsp butter
- ¼ cup of chopped onion
- ½ tsp minced garlic
- 1 cup of aborio rice or other risotto rice
- 1 2/3 cups of chicken broth
- Salt and pepper
- 2 Tbsp extra butter
- 3 Tbsp freshly grated parmesan cheese

Directions

1. Put 2 Tbsp butter, onion and garlic in the rice cooker.
2. Turn the rice cooker to Cook. when the butter is melted let it "cook" an additional 2 mins.
3. Add the arborio rice, stir and cook 10 mins, until the rice is mostly clear with a small white center in each grain.
4. Add broth, salt and pepper, stir and close the lid and reset cooking time, Because there is so much liquid it will take longer to cook than a normal setting so leave yourself extra time.
5. When the machine is done let sit for at least 10 mins or until your ready to serve then stir in the last 1 Tbsp of butter and parmesan.

Nutritional Information

- Calories: 297
- Fat: 16g
- Carbs: 11g
- Protein: 27g

ARTICHOKE MIXED WITH BROWN RICE

Preparation Time: 10 Minutes

Yield: 4 Servings

Ingredients

To Cook in the Rice Cooker:

- 2 cups (rice measuring cup) short or medium grain brown rice
- Water to fill to water level 2 for brown rice

To Prepare Separately:

- 2 Tbsp. olive oil
- 1/2 medium onion, minced
- 2 (14 oz.) canned artichoke hearts in water, drained and chopped
- 1 tsp. salt
- 1/4 tsp. pepper
- 1 lemon zest
- 2 Tbsp. fresh dill, chopped

Directions

1. Add water by filling up to the water scale marked "2" for "Brown Rice". Cook the rice using the "Brown Rice" setting. If your rice cooker does not have a brown rice setting, add 3 cups of water measured in the rice measuring cup.

2. When the rice cooker begins to count down to completion, heat a large frying pan over medium high, add olive oil and onion, and sauté until onion becomes soft, about 5 minutes.
3. Add artichokes and sauté for 3 more minutes.
4. Add cooked brown rice, salt, pepper, lemon zest and mix well until heated through.
5. Turn off the heat and mix in the dill.
6. Serve and enjoy for any meal of the day!

Nutritional Information

- Calories: 297
- Fat: 16g
- Carbs: 11g
- Protein: 27g

ASPARAGUS RICE WITH SEARED SCALLOPS

Preparation Time: 20 Minutes

Yield: 4 Servings

Ingredients

- 1 cup (rice measuring cup) long grain white rice
- 1-1/4 cups (rice measuring cup) water

For Blanching Asparagus:

- 2 quarts water
- 1 Tbsp. salt for blanching water
- 12 oz. fresh asparagus
- 1 clove garlic, peeled
- 1 whole fresh shallot, peeled
- 2 quarts ice water to chill

To Add to Blender:

- 2 Tbsp. whole butter at room temperature

- 1/2 tsp. salt
- Blanching water as needed

To Garnish:

- 1/2 lb. large sea scallops
- 1/2 tsp. salt
- 2 tsp. canola or other neutral flavored vegetable oil

Directions

1. Measure rice accurately using the measuring cup that came with your rice cooker. Rinse rice quickly once, drain and place in the inner cooking pan. Add water and cook the rice using the "Mixed Rice" setting.
2. While the rice is cooking, blanch the asparagus. Boil the water in a saucepan and add 1 Tbsp. of salt. Also prepare 2 quarts ice water. Cut off the hard ends of the asparagus and discard. Cut the tips off the asparagus, about 2 inches, and reserve separately. Chop the remainder of the stalks into short, even pieces.
3. Add the chopped asparagus stalks (but not the tips), garlic and shallot to boiling water and blanch for 1 minute. Remove from boiling water and plunge into ice water to chill thoroughly.
4. Remove chilled asparagus from ice water and place in a blender with salt and softened butter. Puree until mixture is smooth – use a small amount of the blanching water to facilitate smooth blending if needed.
5. Repeat blanching and chilling procedure with asparagus tips; hold tips separately for garnishing.
6. Place oil in a small sauté pan (6-8" diameter) and heat until quite hot, almost smoking. Sprinkle scallops with salt and sear until lightly browned. When scallops are cooked, remove from the pan.
7. Add asparagus tips to the hot pan and toss quickly to heat through.

8. When rice completes cooking, gently fold in the asparagus puree.
9. Serve in bowls and garnish each serving with the scallops and asparagus tips.

Nutritional Information

- Calories: 305
- Fat: 16g
- Carbs: 10g
- Protein: 27g

AVOCADO BOWL WITH YOGURT SAUCE

Preparation Time: 20 Minutes

Yield: 4 Servings

Ingredients

To Cook in the Rice Cooker:

- 2 cups (rice measuring cup) long grain white rice
- 2-1/2 cups (rice measuring cup) water

To Prepare Separately:

- 1-1/2 cups Greek yogurt
- 1/2 tsp. salt
- 1 tsp. honey
- 1 Tbsp. parsley, minced
- 3 ripe avocados, pitted and peeled
- 1 cup heirloom tomatoes, diced

Directions

1. Add water and cook the rice using the "Mixed Rice" setting.
2. In a small bowl, mix yogurt, salt, honey and parsley to make the sauce.
3. Chop avocados into bite-sized pieces.
4. When rice completes cooking, gently fluff the rice using the rice spatula. Serve onto individual bowls and top with yogurt sauce, tomatoes and avocados.
5. Enjoy!

Nutritional Information

- Calories: 250
- Fat: 12g
- Carbs: 8g
- Protein: 25g

BAKED RICE CASSEROLE WITH ARTICHOKES AND MUSHROOMS

Preparation Time: 20 Minutes

Yield: 4 Servings

Ingredients

- 1-1/2 cups (rice measuring cup) long grain white rice
- 1-3/4 cups (rice measuring cup) water
- 1/2 tsp. salt

To Prepare Separately:

- 1/8 cup olive oil
- 4 oz. fresh white mushrooms, quartered
- 3-4 canned or fresh small artichoke hearts, quartered
- 16 oz. prepared mushroom soup, not condensed
- 1/2 tsp. Worcestershire sauce

- 1/2 cup grated parmesan cheese
- 1/4 cup parsley, chopped

Directions

1. Add water and salt to the inner cooking pan and stir well with rice using the rice spatula. Cook the rice using the "Mixed Rice" setting.
2. While the rice cooks, prepare the mushroom and artichoke mixture. In a heavy frying pan, heat olive oil until lightly smoking. Add quartered mushrooms and sauté adjusting heat to keep from scorching until slightly crisp on all sides and golden brown. Reserve in a warm bowl.
3. Sauté artichoke hearts in the same frying pan until crisp and golden brown. Reserve with the mushroom.
4. When the rice cooker begins to countdown to completion, preheat oven to 425°F.
5. In a small sauce pot, heat mushroom soup and Worcestershire sauce over low heat. Be careful not to scorch. When hot, turn off heat and keep warm.
6. In a separate bowl, combine the parmesan cheese and parsley.
7. When rice completes cooking, gently fluff the rice with the rice spatula. Pour in the mushroom soup mixture. Add 1/2 of parmesan cheese and parsley mixture and all of cooked mushrooms and artichokes to the rice. Gently stir to combine and evenly distribute. Place mixed rice in a large oven proof casserole or ceramic bowl.
8. Sprinkle the remaining parmesan cheese and parsley mixture on top of the prepared casserole. Place in the preheated oven and bake for 15 – 20 minutes or until the top of the casserole is golden brown and the mushroom soup is bubbling at the edges.
9. Remove casserole from oven and allow to cool – about 5 minutes. Spoon baked casserole into warm plates and serve immediately.

10. Enjoy!

Nutritional Information

- Calories: 250
- Fat: 12g
- Carbs: 8g
- Protein: 25g

KOREAN RICE BOWL

Preparation Time: 20 Minutes

Yield: 4 Servings

Ingredients

- 2 cups (rice measuring cup) short or medium grain white rice
- Water to fill to water level 2 for white rice

To Prepare Separately:

- 1 cup daikon radish, julienned
- 1/2 bunch spinach
- 2 cups bean sprouts
- 1 cup carrots, julienned
- 1 tsp. sugar
- 1 Tbsp. vinegar
- 1 tsp. soy sauce
- 2 tsps. dark sesame oil
- 1 tsp. salt
- 2 tsps. vegetable oil
- 8 oz. ground beef

Sauce:

- 1 clove garlic, minced
- 2 tsps. sugar

- 2 tsps. soy sauce
- 2 tsps. dark sesame oil

Toppings:

- 4 eggs
- A handful crushed Korean dry seaweed
- 2 tsp. sesame seeds
- Gochuchang (seasoned red pepper paste) to taste

Directions

1. Add water by filling up to the water scale marked "2" for "White Rice". Cook the rice using the "Regular" setting.
2. While rice is cooking, prepare the toppings. Mix 1/4 tsp. salt, sugar and vinegar into daikon radish and set aside.
3. Blanch the spinach. Drain and cool with cold water and squeeze out water. Cut into 3 inch long segments, then dress with 1/4 tsp. salt, soy sauce and 1 tsp. sesame oil.
4. Blanch the bean sprouts. Drain and dress with 1/4 tsp. salt and 1 tsp. sesame oil.
5. In a frying pan, heat vegetable oil over medium heat and sauté carrots for one minute and add 1/4 tsp. salt. Set aside.
6. In a small bowl, combine all ingredients for sauce. Heat frying pan, sauté ground beef for 3 minutes, add the sauce and continue to cook until all the liquid is absorbed.
7. Fry four eggs sunny side up.
8. When rice completes cooking, place rice in individual serving bowls. Squeeze excess liquid from daikon radish. Arrange all prepared vegetables and beef radially on the rice.
9. Place one sunny side up egg in the center on top of each bowl. Top with crushed seaweed and sesame seeds. Serve with gochuchang on the side.

Nutritional Information

- Calories: 523
- Fat: 24g
- Carbs: 15g
- Protein: 32g

WILD RICE AND CHICKEN LIVER CROSTINI

Preparation Time: 20 Minutes

Yield: 4 Servings

Ingredients

- 1 cup (rice measuring cup) wild rice
- 1/4 tsp. salt
- 1/4 tsp. coarse ground black pepper
- 12 oz. water
- 4 fresh sage leaves, whole, do not chop

To Prepare Separately:

- 2 Tbsps. extra virgin olive oil
- 16 oz. onions, chopped
- 24 oz. chicken liver, sliced
- 2 cloves garlic, minced
- 2 Tbsps. fresh sage, chopped
- 2 tsps. salt
- 1/4 tsp. black pepper
- 6 Tbsps. dry sherry
- 1 tsp. red wine vinegar
- For crostini, cut French or Italian bread into 1/3" slices, brush with olive oil and toast until golden brown on both sides

Directions

1. Add salt, pepper and water to the inner cooking pan and mix with rice using the rice spatula. Place whole sage

leaves on top of the rice. Cook the rice using the "Brown Rice" setting.
2. While the rice cooks, prepare the chicken liver combination. In a large sauté pan, heat olive oil until very hot. Add onions and cook until deep, caramel brown.
3. Reduce heat to low and add sliced chicken liver and cook until medium done. Stir to crumble liver into smaller pieces.
4. Add minced garlic, sage, salt, pepper, sherry and vinegar to liver and onion mixture and stir to coarsely combine.
5. When rice completes cooking, discard sage leaves and gently fold liver mixture into rice with rice spatula. Mixture may be made ahead and stored, refrigerated for up to a day.
6. Serve with crostini.

Nutritional Information

- Calories: 326
- Fat: 12g
- Carbs: 8g
- Protein: 23g

SEAWEED MIXED RICE

Preparation Time: 20 Minutes

Yield: 4 Servings

Ingredients

- 1 cup (rice measuring cup) short or medium grain white rice
- Water to fill to water level 1 for white rice

To Prepare Separately:

- 2 Tbsps. wakame seaweed, dried and cut
- 1/2 tsp. salt

- 2 tsps. mirin (Japanese sweet rice wine)
- 1 Tbsp. chives, minced
- 1 tsp. sesame oil
- 2 tsps. sesame seeds

Directions

1. Crush wakame seaweed with your palms to make small flakes.
2. When rice completes cooking, add wakame and all other ingredients to the rice and gently fold in using the rice spatula.
3. Close the lid and let it set for 5 minutes.
4. Serve while hot.

Nutritional Information

- Calories: 192
- Fat: 12g
- Carbs: 8g
- Protein: 7g

TROPICAL LONG GRAIN SALAD

Preparation Time: 20 Minutes

Yield: 4 Servings

Ingredients

- 1 cup (rice measuring cup) long grain white rice
- Water to fill to water level 1 for "Long Grain White"
- 1/4 tsp. salt

To Add to Cooked Rice:

- 1 Tbsp. olive oil

For Dressing:

- 2 Tbsps. orange marmalade
- 2 Tbsps. lime juice
- 1 Tbsp. white wine vinegar
- 1/8 tsp. salt or adjust taste to preference
- 1/8 tsp. pepper
- 1/3 cup olive oil

To Add to Cooked, Cooled Rice:

- 1 lb. extra large cooked shrimp, peeled and deveined
- 1 mango, peeled, diced
- 1/3 cup chopped fresh mint
- 1/3 cup chopped cilantro
- 4 scallions, minced
- 1/4 cup unsweetened shredded coconut, lightly toasted

Directions

1. For 3-cup rice cookers, add water to water level 1 for "Long Grain White", or 1-1/4 cups (rice measuring cup). For 5-10 cup rice cookers, add water to water level 2 for "Long Grain White", or 2-1/2 cups (rice measuring cup). Add salt and mix well. Cook the rice using the "Long Grain White" (if available), or the "Mixed" setting.
2. When rice completes cooking, add olive oil, gently fluff the rice with rice spatula, and spread out onto a large plate. Refrigerate to cool, about 30 minutes.
3. In a bowl, add orange marmalade, lime juice, white wine vinegar, salt, pepper, olive oil and mix well.
4. On a large plate, place rice in the center. Arrange, shrimp, mango, mint, cilantro, scallions, coconut. Pour dressing and toss before serving.

Enjoy!

Nutritional Information

- Calories: 326
- Fat: 5g
- Carbs: 9g
- Protein: 56g

TERIYAKI RICE BURGER

Preparation Time: 20 Minutes

Yield: 4 Servings

Ingredients

- 2 cups (rice measuring cup) short or medium grain white rice
- Water to fill to water level 2 for White Rice
- 1/2 tsp. salt

Chicken Patties:

- 4 oz. tofu, drained
- 1/2 lb. ground chicken
- 1/2 Tbsp. sake (Japanese rice wine)
- 2 cloves garlic, minced
- 2 stalks green onion, minced
- 2 Tbsps. beaten egg
- 1/4 tsp. salt
- 1/4 tsp. ground black pepper
- Potato starch, as needed for dusting (may substitute with cornstarch)
- 2 Tbsp. olive oil

Rice Buns:

- 3 Tbsps. red paprika, diced into 1/4"

- 3 Tbsps. yellow paprika, diced into 1/4"
- 2 Tbsps. jalapeno, minced
- 1 Tbsp. white sesame seeds
- 1/4 tsp. salt
- 1 Tbsp. olive oil

Teriyaki Sauce:

- 3 Tbsps. soy sauce
- 2 Tbsps. sake (Japanese rice wine)
- 1 Tbsp. Mirin (Japanese sweet cooking rice wine)
- 1 Tbsp. sugar
- 1 1/2 Tbsp. honey
- Topping (optional):
- 1/4 cup spring mix leaves
- 5 thinly sliced red onion
- 5 slices tomato
- 5 slices cheese

Directions

1. Measure rice accurately and place in inner cooking pan. Rinse rice under water until water clears. Add water by filling up to the water scale marked "2" for "White Rice," add salt and mix well. Cook the rice using the "White Rice" or "Quick" setting.
2. While rice cooks, place drained tofu in a large bowl and mash with a fork. Add ground chicken, sake, garlic, green onion, egg, salt, pepper and mix well with clean hands.
3. Divide mixture into five 1/2" thick round patties. Slightly dent the center of each patty. Lightly dust with potato starch and set aside.
4. Prepare the teriyaki sauce. Mix all ingredients in a small sauce pan. Simmer over very low heat for 7-8 minutes, skimming the solids from surface until sauce thickens.

Make sure not to overcook or burn the sauce. Remove from heat and set aside.
5. When rice completes cooking, fluff in red paprika, yellow paprika, jalapeño, white sesame seeds and salt using the rice spatula that came with your rice cooker.
6. Divide the rice mixture into two and place one rice mixture in a gallon size 10" x 14" plastic bag. Spread into a square, slightly mashing the rice.
7. Using a rolling pin over the bag, roll and thin out rice mixture into 1/2" thickness. Using a 3" circle cookie cutter or empty can, cut out the rice buns over the plastic bag. Repeat steps 6 and 7 to cut out a total of 10 buns. (Gather and re-roll leftover rice mixture and repeat if necessary.)
8. Heat 1/2 Tbsp. olive oil in a frying pan over medium-low heat. Place 5 rice buns and cook for 3-4 minutes each side or until both sides are toasty and crispy. Set aside on a cooling rack. Heat another 1/2 Tbsp. olive oil and repeat for the rest of the rice buns.
9. Cook the chicken patties. Heat 2 Tbsp. olive oil in a frying pan over medium-low heat, and place prepared patties. Cover lid and brown both sides, approximately 3-5 minutes each side or until cooked through.
10. Please be careful of the heated pan and splashing oil. Wipe the lid of moisture and oil when flipping patties.
11. Run each cooked patty through the prepared teriyaki sauce, and assemble the burger. Add spring mix leaves, sliced red onion, tomato and cheese if preferred. Serve immediately.

Nutritional Information

- Calories: 209
- Fat: 7g
- Carbs: 18g
- Protein: 22g

5. Appetizers and Side Dishes

Tuna & Avocado Plate

Preparation Time: 10 Minutes

Yield: 4 Servings

Ingredients

- 2 cups sushi rice, cooked
- 2 avocados, pitted, peeled, and cut into 1/2-inch cubes
- 1/4 cup freshly squeezed lemon juice
- 8 oz. fresh sashimi quality tuna, cut into 1/2-inch cubes
- Salad or sprouts as garnish (optional)

Directions

1. Prepare the sushi rice.
2. Add lemon juice to cubed avocados.
3. Lay plastic wrap on the bottom of the ramekins.
4. Spread 1/4 of the avocados from step 2 in an even layer on the bottom of the ramekin.
5. Over avocado, spread about 2 ounces of cubed tuna.
6. Top with 1/2 cup of sushi rice.
7. Use the bottom of another ramekin to press the rice. Repeat steps 3 to 7 for all the ramekins.
8. Turn the ramekin upside down onto a plate, so the rice layer is on the bottom.
9. Serve garnished with salad or sprouts.

Nutritional Information

- Calories: 270
- Fat: 7g
- Carbs: 15g

- Protein: 22g

THAI GREEN CHICKEN CURRY

Preparation Time: 20 Minutes

Yield: 4 Servings

Ingredients

- 2 cups (rice measuring cup) Jasmine rice
- Water to fill to water level 2 for "Jasmine Rice" or 2 1/2 cups (rice measuring cup) water

For Paste:

- 1/4 tsp. cumin seeds, toasted
- 1/2 tsp. coriander seeds, toasted
- 1/4 tsp. white peppercorns, toasted
- 1 stalk lemongrass, white part only, thinly chopped
- 1 Tbsp. galangal (may substitute with ginger), chopped
- 1 small shallot, chopped
- 1 Tbsp. garlic, chopped
- 10 prik kee noo (Thai green chili pepper) (may substitute with small green chilies of your choice), chopped, adjust amount for preferred hotness
- 1/2 kaffir lime peel (may substitute with lime peel)
- 1 kaffir lime leaf, torn (optional)
- 1/2 tsp. kapi (Thai shrimp paste) (optional)
- 2 Tbsps. fresh coriander roots, chopped
- 10 Thai basil leaves (may substitute with basil leaves), chopped
- 1/2 tsp. sea salt

For Curry:

- 1 lb. boneless and skinless chicken breast, cut into bite-sized pieces
- 1-1/2 Tbsp. fish sauce
- 1 (14 oz.) can coconut milk
- 1 cup chicken stock
- 3-4 Thai eggplants (may substitute with small Asian eggplants), cut into bite-sized pieces
- 1 (8 oz.) can of sliced bamboo shoots, drained
- 2 tsps. palm sugar (may substitute with light brown sugar)
- 3 fresh kaffir lime leaves, torn (optional)
- 4 sprigs Thai basil leaves (may substitute with basil leaves), reserve stem for garnish

Directions

1. Measure the rice accurately using the measuring cup that came with your rice cooker. Rinse quickly once, drain and place in the inner cooking pan.
2. Add water by filling up to the water scale marked "2" for "Jasmine Rice" or add water. Cook the rice using the "Jasmine" or "White Rice" setting.
3. Using a hand blender or a table-top blender, blend all ingredients for "For Paste". Add water if necessary.
4. Place chicken breast in a bowl, mix 1/2 tablespoon of fish sauce, cover and set aside.
5. In a large sauce pan, place half of coconut milk and cook over medium heat until water evaporates and the amount is reduced to half or until the oil surfaces, about 6 to 8 minutes.
6. Add the paste from step 3 and stir, cooking until fragrant, about 3 minutes.
7. Add the chicken, remaining coconut milk, chicken stock, eggplants, bamboo shoots, remaining fish sauce, sugar and lime leaves. Bring it to a boil and simmer for 10 minutes.

8. When the chicken pieces are cooked and eggplants are tender, stir in prik chee far daeng, adjust taste to your preference with fish sauce (not included in the ingredients list) and turn heat off. Reserve stems of the basil leaves for garnish, add leaves to the curry and mix.
9. When rice completes cooking, gently fluff the rice using the rice spatula and serve onto individual plates.
10. Serve curry with rice, garnish with basil stems.
11. Enjoy while hot!

Nutritional Information

- Calories: 400
- Fat: 17g
- Carbs: 12g
- Protein: 31g

TEMPURA BOWL

Preparation Time: 20 Minutes

Yield: 4 Servings

Ingredients

- 2 cups (rice measuring cup) short or medium grain white rice
- Water to fill to water level 2 for white rice

To Prepare Separately:

- 4 servings Tempura, battered with 2 Tbsp. extra flour

Sauce:

- 6 Tbsp. soy sauce
- 4 Tbsp. mirin (Japanese sweet rice wine)

- 2 Tbsp. sugar

Directions

1. Measure the rice accurately and place in the inner cooking pan. Rinse rice under water until water clears.
2. Add water by filling up to the water scale marked "2" for "White Rice". Cook the rice using the "Regular" setting.
3. Make Tempura in a thicker batter by adding an extra 2 Tbsp. of flour to the batter and keep warm.
4. In a small saucepan, put soy sauce, mirin, sugar and bring to a simmer over medium heat.
5. When rice completes cooking, fill each serving bowl with rice and top with Tempura. Drizzle the prepared sauce and serve immediately.

Nutritional Information

- Calories: 400
- Fat: 17g
- Carbs: 12g
- Protein: 31g

TEMARI SUSHI

Preparation Time: 10 Minutes

Yield: 4 Servings

Ingredients

For Sushi Rice:

- 2 cups sushi rice
- 3 Tbsp. rice vinegar
- 1-1/2 Tbsp. sugar
- 1/2 tsp. salt

Other Ingredients:

- 10 edamame beans, frozen and shelled
- 5 medium shrimp, deveined and precooked
- 1 Tbsp. rice vinegar
- 2 Tbsp. water
- 1/8 tsp. salt
- 5 slices smoked salmon (about 5 oz.)
- 1 green onion

Garnish and Condiments:

- Soy sauce
- Wasabi paste
- Gari (pickled ginger)

Directions

1. Prepare sushi rice using the ingredients listed.
2. Preheat other ingredients. Blanch edamame and place in cold water. Remove tails of shrimp and slice in half lengthwise.
3. Mix rice vinegar, water and salt in a bowl. Place drained edamame and sliced shrimp in the bowl and soak for 15 minutes to up to 6 hours in the refrigerator.
4. Cut smoked salmon slices in halves and mince green onion. Set aside.
5. Divide prepared sushi rice in half for the shrimp temari and smoked salmon temari.
6. Cut a large square of plastic wrap and place on a flat surface.
7. Place one piece of salmon at the center of the plastic wrap.
8. Place a bite sized scoop of sushi rice on top of the salmon. Gather the plastic wrap up around the rice ball, then twist the plastic wrap and make a ball shape.

9. Make a small indentation on top and place on the serving plate, rice side down. Then remove wrap.
10. Repeat steps 6 to 9 and make ten salmon temari-sushi pieces.
11. Make 10 pieces of shrimp temari-sushi using same steps as the salmon temari.
12. Top with minced green onion for salmon temari, top with edamame for shrimp temari.
13. Serve both with soy sauce, wasabi and gari. Enjoy!

Nutritional Information

- Calories: 100
- Fat: 5g
- Carbs: 6g
- Protein: 2g

SHRIMP **S**TIR-**F**RIED **R**ICE

Preparation Time: 20 Minutes

Yield: 4 Servings

Ingredients

- 3 cups (rice measuring cup) short or medium grain white or brown rice
- Water to fill to water level 3 for white or brown rice

To Prepare Separately:

- 3 Tbsp. vegetable oil
- 4 large eggs, lightly beaten
- 2 large garlic cloves, minced
- 3 scallions, both green and white parts, cut thin diagonally
- 10 oz. small shrimp, cleaned, shelled, frozen or fresh, cut into half diagonally

- 1 tsp. sea salt
- 2/3 cup frozen edamame soybeans or green peas, cooked in boiling water for 1 minute, cooled under cold tap water and drained
- 2 to 3 tsp. soy sauce
- 1/2 tsp. white pepper powder or freshly ground black peppercorns

Directions

1. Measure the rice accurately and place in the inner cooking pan. Rinse white rice under water until water clears, or just once if using brown rice.
2. Add water by filling up to the water scale marked "3" for "White Rice" or "Brown Rice," whichever you are using. Cook the rice using the "Harder" or "Regular" setting for white rice, and "Brown Rice" setting for brown rice.
3. When rice completes cooking, transfer the rice to a strainer and rinse under cold tap water to cool the rice and remove excess starch. Drain the rice and let stand 20 minutes before stir-frying. When using rice that has been previously cooked and stored in the refrigerator, omit this step.
4. Heat 2 Tbsp. of vegetable oil in a wok or a large skillet and cook the eggs over moderately high heat. When the bottom of the eggs become firm, give several large stirs with a spatula and transfer the egg to a bowl. At this stage, the egg is still tender and is a mixture of the firm cooked part and runny part.
5. Add the remaining 1 Tbsp. of vegetable oil to the wok or skillet and cook the garlic and scallion until fragrant over high heat, about 20 seconds. Add the shrimp and salt and cook until the outsides of the shrimp are white, stirring the mixture continuously with a spatula.

6. Add the rinsed or cold rice and cook heated through, stirring continuously with a spatula. Add the green peas or soybeans and cook until heated through. Add the reserved eggs. Season with shoyu and white or black peppercorn.
7. Divide and serve in 4 to 6 bowls while hot.

Nutritional Information

- Calories: 244
- Fat: 10g
- Carbs: 15g
- Protein: 16g

SHIITAKE MUSHROOM RICE

Preparation Time: 20 Minutes

Yield: 4 Servings

Ingredients

To Prepare in Advance:

- 5 medium dried shiitake mushrooms
- 1 cup water to soak shiitake (reserve)
- 2 Tbsp. sake (rice wine)
- 2 Tbsp. shoyu (soy sauce)
- 2 Tbsp. mirin (Japanese sweet sake)

To Cook in the Rice Cooker:

- 3 cups (rice measuring cup) short or medium grain white rice
- Water to fill to water level 3 for white rice

To Prepare Separately:

- Stone parsley to taste

- Sliced ginger to taste

Directions

1. Soak the shiitake mushroom in water for 30 minutes to an hour to reconstitute. Reserve the stock. Slice the shiitake and cook briefly in the reserved stock, sake, shoyu and mirin.
2. Measure rice accurately and place in inner cooking pan. Rinse rice under water until water clears. Add the stock from step 1 and add water by filling up to the water scale marked "3" for "White Rice" for 5 and 10 cup rice cookers, and up to "1.5" for 3 cup rice cookers.
3. Add the cooked shiitake from step 1, and mix well. Cook the rice using the "Mixed" setting.
4. When rice completes cooking, open the lid and fluff the rice to loosen and serve.
5. Top with chopped stone parsley and sliced ginger.

Nutritional Information

- Calories: 223
- Fat: 15g
- Carbs: 15g
- Protein: 16g

SALSA VERDE STYLE BROWN RICE

Preparation Time: 10 Minutes

Yield: 4 Servings

Ingredients

To Cook in the Rice Cooker:

- 2 cups (rice measuring cup) short grain brown rice
- Water to fill to water level 2 for brown rice

To Prepare Separately:

- 12 oz. fresh or frozen spinach
- 1/4 cup water from cooking or defrosting spinach, or as needed
- 1 shallot, peeled
- 1 clove garlic, peeled
- 2 Tbsps. capers in brine, drained
- 1 Tbsp. fresh parsley, chopped
- 1 Tbsp. fresh tarragon, chopped
- 1/4 cup Parmesan cheese, grated
- 4 canned anchovy filets

For Garnish:

- 1-2 oz. Grating cheese such as Ricotta salata cheese

Directions

1. Measure rice accurately using the measuring cup that came with your rice cooker and place in the inner cooking pan. Rinse quickly once and drain.
2. Add water to the inner cooking pan and cook the rice using the "Brown Rice" setting.
3. While rice cooks, prepare the salsa verde mixture. Cook fresh spinach in rapidly boiling salted water (not included in ingredient list). If using frozen spinach, defrost in a microwave. Reserve 1/4 cup of spinach water for blending.
4. In a blender, add spinach, spinach water and all other ingredients except garnish and puree until smooth.
5. Pour pureed sauce into a sauce pot and heat gently to warm the sauce. Keep warm until rice completes cooking.
6. When rice completes cooking, add sauce to rice and gently combine using the rice spatula.
7. Spoon into individual serving bowls and garnish with grated cheese. Serve while hot.

8. Enjoy!

Nutritional Information

- Calories: 100
- Fat: 15g
- Carbs: 8g
- Protein: 8g

Salmon Teriyaki with Mixed Vegetables over Rice

Preparation Time: 20 Minutes

Yield: 4 Servings

Ingredients

- 3 cups (rice measuring cup) short or medium grain white or brown rice
- Water to fill to water level 3 for white rice or brown rice

To Prepare Separately:

Sauce:

- 1 cup mirin (Japanese sweet rice wine)
- 1/2 cup sake (rice wine)
- 1/2 cup shoyu (soy sauce)
- 1/4 cup sugar
- 4 garlic cloves
- 1 tsp. Italian hot dried chile flakes
- 1 1/4 lbs. salmon with skin, cut into 4 to 6 pieces
- 2 1/8 tsps. Sea salt
- 1 Tbsp. Vegetable oil
- 2 cups of frozen mixed vegetables
- 1 Tbsp. white sesame seeds

Directions

1. Add water by filling up to the water scale marked "3" for "White Rice" or "Brown Rice," whichever you are using. Cook the rice using the "Harder" or "Regular" setting for white rice, and "Brown Rice" setting for brown rice.
2. In a small saucepan heat the mirin and sake until it comes to simmer over medium heat. Add the sugar and shoyu and bring it to a gentle simmer, dissolving the sugar. Turn the heat to low, add the garlic and cook the mixture for 7 minutes. Turn off the heat, add the chile flakes and cool to room temperature.
3. Salt the salmon pieces with 1 tsp. salt on each side and let it stand for 20 minutes. Rinse the salmon under cold tap water, drain and gently wipe dry the fish with paper towel. Heat a nonstick or regular skillet over medium heat. Apply a thin coating of oil to the bottom of the skillet. Salt the salmon with 1/8 tsp. salt and place the fish in the skillet, skin-side down. Cook the salmon over medium-low heat until the skin is golden. Turn over the fish and cook it over low heat, until fish is almost cooked through, about 7 minutes. Spoon 6 to 8 Tbsps. prepared sauce evenly over each fish and let the sauce sizzle in the skillet. Be careful not burn the sauce. Turn off the heat.
4. Divide and transfer the cooked rice in 4 to 6 bowls. Spoon 1 tablespoon prepared sauce over the rice. Top each rice portion with a salmon piece. Divide and pour the leftover sauce in the skillet over the fish. Clean the skillet.
5. Put the skillet back on the stove and heat it over high heat. Add the vegetable oil, and when the oil sizzles, add the frozen mixed vegetables. Cook the vegetables over high heat, stirring all the time, for 1 to 2 minutes. Remove the skillet from the heat and add 1 to 2 Tbsp. prepared sauce. Put the skillet back to the heat and toss the vegetables with the sauce.

6. Divide the cooked vegetables next to the fish in the 4 to 6 bowls. Garnish each bowl with white sesame seeds and serve.

Nutritional Information

- Calories: 320
- Fat: 15g
- Carbs: 14g
- Protein: 30g

RICE SPRINKLES ONIGIRI

Preparation Time: 20 Minutes

Yield: 4 Servings

Ingredients

- 2 cups (rice measuring cup) short or medium grain white rice
- Water to fill to water level 2 for White Rice

For Vegetable Furikake:

- 1 Tbsp. sesame oil
- 1 small carrot, diced
- 1/3 cup daikon, diced
- 2 cups kale leaves, chopped into small pieces
- 1 Tbsp. shoyu (soy sauce)
- 1 Tbsp. mirin (Japanese sweet rice wine)
- 1/2 tsp. sugar
- 1/4 tsp. salt
- 1 tsp. toasted white sesame seeds

Directions

1. Prepare white rice.

2. While rice cooks, make furikake. Heat sesame oil in a frying pan over medium heat. Add carrot, daikon, kale to the pan and sauté for 3 minutes.
3. Add shoyu, mirin, sugar, salt to the pan and sauté more 3 minutes or until liquid is almost evaporated, then add sesame seeds.
4. When rice completes cooking, transfer rice to another bowl, sprinkle furikake from step 3 and gently fold with the rice spatula.
5. Cut and place a plastic wrap about 7 to 8 inches long and place in a small bowl. Add 1/8 of mixed rice on top of the plastic wrap. Gather the plastic wrap around the rice and make a triangular rice ball by squeezing your hands together lightly. The rice ball should be firm so it does not fall apart, but the rice should remain fluffy and not smashed. Repeat this step to make seven more onigiri.
6. Remove plastic wraps from onigiri and plate.
7. Enjoy!

Nutritional Information

- Calories: 220
- Fat: 5g
- Carbs: 30g
- Protein: 6g

RICE OMELET

Preparation Time: 20 Minutes

Yield: 4 Servings

Ingredients

- 1 lb. cooked rice, warm, about 1-1/2 cups raw
- 4 oz. chicken thigh, boneless
- 5 mushrooms

- 2 Tbsps. butter
- 2 oz. onion, chopped
- 3 Tbsps. ketchup
- 1/4 cup chicken broth
- 1/2 tsp. salt
- 1/4 tsp. pepper
- 4 eggs
- 2 Tbsps. milk
- 2 Tbsps. vegetable oil

For Sauce:

- 1/4 cup ketchup
- 1 Tbsp. Worcestershire sauce

Directions

1. Dice chicken into small pieces, and slice mushrooms.
2. Heat butter in skillet over medium-high heat and sauté chicken, onion and mushroom for 3 minutes.
3. Add 3 Tbsps. ketchup, chicken broth, salt, pepper and continue to cook until liquid evaporates.
4. Add cooked warm rice to the skillet and mix well. Remove the chicken rice from the pan and set aside.
5. In a bowl, mix eggs and milk.
6. Wipe skillet and heat 1 Tbsp. oil over medium heat, making sure entire surface of pan is coated. Pour half of egg mixture into the pan.
7. Move a spatula through the egg mixture in circular motion until the egg is half way cooked through.
8. Place half of chicken rice in the center of the egg mixture and turn the heat off.
9. Tilt the skillet to the side a bit and fold one side of egg over the rice. Push and slide omelet to the other side of the skillet.

10. When the omelet reaches the edge of the skillet, flip it out onto a serving plate so the sides of the egg folds under the rice.
11. If necessary use a paper towel to correct the shape. Repeat steps 6-11 to make another omelet.
12. Combine ketchup and Worcestershire sauce in a small bowl and pour over each omelet.
13. Serve hot.

Nutritional Information

- Calories: 250
- Fat: 16g
- Carbs: 15g
- Protein: 8g

6. Dairy Recipes

Chicken Bacon Chowder

Preparation Time: 40 Minutes

Yield: 4 Servings

Ingredients

- 4 cloves garlic, minced
- 1 shallot, finely chopped
- 1 small leek, cleaned, trimmed and sliced
- 2 ribs celery, diced
- 6 oz cremini mushrooms, sliced
- 1 medium sweet onion, thinly sliced
- 4 tbsps butter, divided
- 2 cups chicken stock
- 1 lb chicken breasts
- 8 oz cream cheese
- 1 cup heavy cream
- 1 lb bacon, cooked crisp and crumbled
- 1 tsp sea salt
- 1 tsp black pepper
- 1 tsp garlic powder
- 1 tsp dried thyme

Directions

1. Heat cooker, add garlic, shallot, leek, celery, mushrooms, onions, 2 tbsp butter, 1 cup chicken stock, sea salt and black pepper. Cover, and cook vegetables.
2. Complete this next step while the vegetables are cooking – In a large skillet over medium-high heat, pan-sear the

chicken breasts in the remaining 2 tbsps of butter until they are browned on both sides. – About 5 minutes each side. (Chicken will not be fully cooked during this stage.)
3. Remove chicken from pan and set aside. De-glaze the pan with the remaining 1 cup of chicken stock. Using a rubber spatula, scrape up any bits of chicken that may be stuck to the pan. Add chicken stock to cooker.
4. Add heavy cream, cream cheese, garlic powder, and thyme to the cooker. Stir until well combined and there are no longer any visible chunks of cream cheese.
5. Once the chicken has cooled, cut it into cubes and add it to the cooker, along with bacon. Stir until all ingredients are well combined. Cover and let cook for 40 minutes.

Nutritional Information

- Calories: 355
- Fat: 28g
- Carbs: 6g
- Protein: 21g

Chicken Cordon Bleu Soup

Preparation Time: 30 Minutes

Yield: 4 Servings

Ingredients

- 6 cups chicken stock
- 12 ounces diced ham
- 5 ounces mushrooms, chopped
- 4 ounces onion, diced
- 2 teaspoons dried tarragon
- 1 teaspoon sea salt, more to taste
- 1 teaspoon black pepper

- 1 pound chicken breast, cubed
- 4 cloves garlic, minced
- 3 tablespoons salted butter
- 1 1/2 cups heavy cream
- 1/2 cup sour cream
- 1/2 cup grated Parmesan cheese
- 4 ounces Swiss cheese

Directions

1. Heat the cooker on the low setting.
2. To the cooker, add the chicken stock, ham, mushrooms, onion, tarragon, salt and pepper. Cover and let cook.
3. In a large saute pan, over medium-high heat, pan-sear the chicken in butter and garlic until browned. Add the chicken, along with all drippings from the pan to the cooker.
4. Next, add the heavy cream, sour cream, Parmesan cheese, and Swiss cheese. Cover and cook for 40 minutes.

Nutritional Information

- Calories: 178
- Fat: 12g
- Carbs: 2g
- Protein: 16g

MEXICAN CHICKEN SOUP

Preparation Time: 20 Minutes

Yield: 4 Servings

Ingredients

- 1 1/2 pounds of chicken pieces boneless/skinless
- 15.5 ounces chunky salsa (I used Tostitos)

- 15 ounces chicken bone broth
- 8 ounces Monterey or Pepper Jack cheese cubed small or shredded

Directions

1. Place chicken pieces at the bottom of your cooker pot.
2. Add remaining ingredients.
3. Cook for 20 minutes
4. Remove chicken pieces and shred chicken. Return to crock.
5. Serve hot.

Nutritional Information

- Calories: 331
- Fat: 23g
- Carbs: 5g
- Protein: 25g

GARLIC BUTTER CHICKEN WITH CREAM CHEESE SAUCE

Preparation Time: 20 Minutes

Yield: 4 Servings

Ingredients

For the garlic chicken:

- 2- 2.5 lbs of chicken breasts
- 1 stick of butter
- 8 garlic cloves sliced in half to release flavor
- 1.5 tsp salt
- Optional -- 1 sliced onion

For the cream cheese sauce:

- 8 oz of cream cheese
- 1 cup of chicken stock
- salt to taste

Directions

For the garlic chicken:

1. Place the chicken (thawed) in the cooker.
2. Add the butter to the cooker.
3. Place the garlic in the cooker, dispersing it around so that it's not all in one spot.
4. Sprinkle with salt.
5. Cook for 20 minutes.
6. Remove and place on serving platter.

For the cream cheese sauce:

1. In a pan, put the cup of chicken stock (or liquid from the cooker).
2. Add the cream cheese and salt.
3. Cook over medium-low heat until the sauce is combined and creamy.
4. Pour over chicken.

Nutritional Information

- Calories: 169
- Fat: 1g
- Carbs: 9g
- Protein: 27g

CHICKEN TIKKA MASALA

Preparation Time: 30 Minutes

Yield: 4 Servings

Ingredients

- 2 lbs boneless skinless chicken breast
- 1 small onion, chopped
- 1/2 yellow bell pepper, chopped
- 2 tablespoons butter or ghee
- 1 teaspoon cumin
- 1 teaspoon coriander
- 2 teaspoons garam masala
- 1 teaspoon turmeric
- 1/4 teaspoon cayenne pepper (or more to taste)
- 1 1/2 teaspoon sea salt
- 15 oz can diced tomatoes
- 1/2 cup full fat coconut milk
- 3 cloves garlic, minced
- 1 teaspoon grated fresh ginger

Directions

1. Set your cooker to Saute. Add butter, onion, and yellow peppers and cook for 3-4 minutes until vegetables start to soften.
2. Add garlic, ginger, spices and salt and cook for an additional 1-2 minutes.
3. Add tomatoes and coconut milk and stir well to combine. Place chicken on top of mixture. Close the lid and set to Poultry (or Manual setting for 15 minutes).
4. When cycle is complete, remove chicken and shred. Using an immersion hand blender, puree the sauce. Add the chicken back to the sauce and adjust seasoning to taste.

Nutritional Information

- Calories: 280
- Fat: 13g
- Carbs: 6g
- Protein: 33g

Buffalo Chicken Meatballs

Preparation Time: 30 Minutes

Yield: 4 Servings

Ingredients

- 1.5 lb ground chicken
- 3/4 cup almond meal
- 1 tsp sea salt
- 2 garlic cloves minced
- 2 green onions thinly sliced
- 2 tbsp ghee
- 6 tbsp hot sauce
- 4 tbsp ghee or butter
- Chopped green onions, for garnish

Directions

1. In a large bowl, combine chicken, almond meal, salt, minced garlic cloves, and green onions.
2. Use your hands to combine everything together, but be careful not to overwork the meat.
3. Grease your hands with ghee or coconut oil, then shape the meat into balls 1-2 inches wide.
4. Set your cooker to sauté setting and add 2 tbsp of ghee.
5. Working in batches, gently place the chicken meatballs in the cooker to brown them. Turn them every minute until all sides are brown.
6. While the meatballs are browning, combine hot sauce and 4 tbsp of butter or ghee and heat them in the microwave or the stove top until the butter is completely melted. Use a spoon to stir. This is your buffalo sauce.
7. Place all the browned meatballs in the cooker, then pour the buffalo sauce evenly over the meatballs.

8. Screw on the lid to the cooker, make sure that the pressure valve is set to "sealing," then set it to "Poultry."
9. Once the meatballs are finished cooking (about 15-20 minutes), the cooker will beep. If you are eating right away, hit "Cancel" then release the pressure valve, making sure your hand is away from the opening where the steam escapes. If not, the cooker will automatically switch to the "Warm" setting for the next 10 hours and the pressure will slowly lower on its own.
10. Serve over rice, cauliflower rice, zoodles. or just eat on its own!

Nutritional Information

- Calories: 357
- Fat: 28g
- Carbs: 3g
- Protein: 23g

COCONUT CHICKEN

Preparation Time: 20 Minutes

Yield: 4 Servings

Ingredients

- 1 bunch of celery, chopped
- 1 pound chicken tenders (or cubed chicken breast)
- 1 cup chicken broth
- 5 stalks lemongrass
- 1 cup full-fat coconut milk
- salt and pepper, to taste
- cooked rice, fresh limes, and sliced scallions (optional), for serving

Directions

1. Add the celery to the cooker. Place the chicken tenders on top of the celery. Add the chicken broth and lemongrass and lock on the Pot lid.
2. Cook on high pressure for 22 minutes and use the quick release to let off the steam.
3. Use tongs to remove the lemongrass and discard.
4. Pour in the coconut milk and give the soup a good stir. Season with salt and pepper, to taste.
5. Serve with cooked rice or cauliflower rice, fresh lime, and sliced scallions, if desired.

Nutritional Information

- Calories: 260
- Fat: 15g
- Carbs: 3g
- Protein: 27g

CAULIFLOWER MASHED POTATOES

Preparation Time: 20 Minutes

Yield: 4 Servings

Ingredients

- 1 large head of cauliflower, cored and cut into large florets
- 1 cup of water
- Rice cooker trivet or a steamer basket
- 1/2 cup butter (optional)
- salt, pepper, garlic power (optional / to taste)

Directions

1. Core your cauliflower and cut into large chunks
2. Add trivet/steamer basket, water, and cauliflower to the Rice cooker

3. Close lid, set valve to sealing
4. Cook on Manual high pressure for 3 to 5 minutes, less for a firmer mash
5. Immediately quick release the pressure and open the lid
6. Carefully remove the inner pot to drain water from
7. Return cauliflower to a cleaned and empty inner pot
8. Add butter and seasonings
9. Use immersion blender to puree until desired consistency is reached
10. Stir, serve, and enjoy!

Nutritional Information

- Calories: 260
- Fat: 15g
- Carbs: 3g
- Protein: 27g

CHUNKY CHILI

Preparation Time: 30 Minutes

Yield: 4 Servings

Ingredients

- 1 ¼ lb ground beef
- 1 tbsp olive oil
- ½ medium sized yellow onion chopped
- 2 cloves garlic peeled and minced
- 1 ½ tbsp chili powder
- 2 tsp cumin
- 1 ½ tsp sea salt
- 1 tsp smoked paprika
- 1 tsp garlic powder
- ¼ tsp coriander powder

- ⅛ tsp cayenne pepper
- 1 cup beef broth
- ⅔ cup water
- ¼ cup canned pumpkin unsweetened kind
- 1 cup canned diced tomatoes
- 2 tbsp tomato paste
- ⅔ cup cauliflower finely chopped
- 1 cup zucchini squash diced
- Toppings:
- ⅔ cup grated cheddar cheese optional
- ½ of an avocado chopped
- 3 tbsp sour cream optional

Directions

1. Select Saute and once the cooker is hot add olive oil and crumble the ground beef into the cooker. Sauté ground beef for 6 minutes, or until beef is browned while using a wooden spoon to stir and break up the beef.
2. Once the beef has browned, add the chopped onions and minced garlic and saute until translucent.
3. Add all the remaining ingredients except for the toppings to the cooker and stir to combine.
4. Close and secure the lid and turn the pressure release handle to the Sealing position. Select Pressure Cook (Manual) on High Pressure and set the timer for 25 minutes.
5. Once cooking time is complete, let pressure naturally release for 10 minutes (do nothing to the cooker for 10 minutes) and then carefully Quick Release all the remaining pressure (turn pressure release to Venting). Let all the pressure (steam) release.
6. Open the lid, stir and serve topped with cheese, chopped avocado and a ½ tbsp of sour cream or paleo sour cream.

Nutritional Information

- Calories: 420
- Fat: 32g
- Carbs: 8g
- Protein: 22g

GHEE **R**ICE

Preparation Time: 20 Minutes

Yield: 4 Servings

Ingredients

- 2 cups Basmati or Long Grain Rice
- 4 cups water – room temperature
- 2 Tbsp Ghee /Clarified Butter + 4 Tbsp For frying the garnish
- 1 ½ tsp salt
- 8 cloves
- 8 green cardamom
- 4 small sticks of cinnamon
- ¼ piece of star anise
- 1 Onion Sliced finely
- $1/8$ tsp (very little) minced garlic- this gives the aroma a boost.
- a couple of squirts of fresh lime juice
- Shallots, sliced finely, Cashewnuts and Golden Raisins – For garnish.

Directions

1. Wash rice. Soak 5 minutes. Drain well for 20 minutes.
2. Heat ghee in your in your rice cooker pot. (On 'Cook' mode)
3. Add the whole spices. Allow to crackle.

4. When aromatic, add the minced garlic. Stir once till softened- do not turn brown.
5. Add the sliced onion. Stir well.
6. Close the rice cooker and allow to go to 'WARM' setting. (Open and stir a few times if needed). Switch the power off and wait for a few minutes. The onions will be golden now.
7. Turn the rice cooker on again – Place on 'Cook' Mode. When the mixture has warmed up again, add the drained rice.
8. Stir well, tossing gently in the golden onion mixture till all the grains are glossed with ghee.
9. Close the cooker and allow to go to 'Warm' setting again. Turn the power off again. Wait a minute.
10. Open the rice cooker and add the water and salt. Bring to a simmer, closed. Also add a few squirts of lime juice. Close the rice cooker again until the light indicates 'WARM'.
11. Once the cooker light indicates 'WARM' again, ie., the cooking is done, switch off the power, so that rice does not get crisp on the bottom. Leave closed for 5 minutes. Then open and fluff up gently with a fork, from the bottom of the rice cooker. Fluffy light Ghee rice is ready.
12. Place in serving platter and garnish with the fried ingredients as desired.

Nutritional Information

- Calories: 420
- Fat: 32g
- Carbs: 8g
- Protein: 22g

7. Soups and Stews

Taco Soup

Preparation Time: 60 Minutes

Yield: 4 Servings

Ingredients

- 1/2 medium – onion
- 1 clove – garlic
- 1 tablespoon – olive oil
- 1 pound – chicken breast
- 5 cup – chicken broth, low-sodium
- 14.5 ounce – diced tomatoes, canned
- 1/2 cup – brown rice, raw
- 1 cup – corn, canned
- 2 medium – carrot
- 1/2 cup – black beans, canned

Directions

1. Chop an onion and garlic, and put it at the bottom of a HOT rice cooker with some oil to get it to start browning.
2. While the rice cooker is heating up the onions and garlic, dice your chicken.
3. Add chicken to rice cooker and cook until browned.
4. Add chicken broth, diced tomatoes, brown rice, and drained corn. Drain and rinse black beans, peel and dice carrots; add to cooker.
5. Turn rice cooker on to "brown rice" setting, if yours has one. Otherwise, turn it on for at least 45 minutes-1 hour.

Nutritional Information

- Calories: 262
- Fat: 8g
- Carbs: 20g
- Protein: 22g

BEEF MINESTRONE SOUP

Preparation Time: 20 Minutes

Yield: 4 Servings

Ingredients

- 2 cans 12 oz each beef chunk
- 2 cans mixed vegetables, such as veg all's
- 1 can green beans
- 1 can petite diced tomatoes or whole tomatoes
- 32 oz beef broth
- 2 Tbsp beef bouillon granules or 2 cubes bouillon cubes crushed

Directions

1. Add all the above to a rice cooker (mine is a 10 cup) and set to white rice. in the time it takes for the rice to be done the soup will be done. You can also add barley or rice or pasta to this for a heavier soup!
2. If you want this vegetarian omit the cans of beef cubes and change the bouillon to 32 oz of vegetable broth. Then add barley, rice or quinoa for a meal type soup!

Nutritional Information

- Calories: 237
- Fat: 14g
- Carbs: 20g
- Protein: 10g

Macaroni Soup

Preparation Time: 30 Minutes

Yield: 4 Servings

Ingredients

- Macaroni x 1/4 cups
- Chicken stock/ water x 2 1/2 cup
- Shredded chicken x 1/4 cup
- Carrot, small x 1
- Tomato, small x 1
- Onion, small x 1
- Potato, small x 1
- Salt to taste (Suggestion: 1 tsp salt)
- Black pepper to taste
- Spring onions (optional)

Directions

1. Gather all ingredients and tools.
2. Wash produce.
3. Chop carrot, potato, tomato and onions into 1 cm cubes. Add into rice cooker pot.
4. Add shredded chicken, macaroni and chicken stock into rice cooker pot.
5. Press cook. You can stop it from cooking and turn the function to keep warm when the pot is bubbling (i.e steam coming out of the pot). About 20 – 30 minutes.
6. Season with salt and pepper.
7. Dish out and enjoy!

Nutritional Information

- Calories: 156
- Fat: 4g

- Carbs: 15g
- Protein: 7g

RICE COOKER DHAL

Preparation Time: 20 Minutes

Yield: 4 Servings

Ingredients

- 2 Tbs. coconut oil
- 1 small yellow onion, finely chopped (1 cup)
- 6 cloves garlic, minced (2 Tbs.)
- 1/2 cup finely chopped carrots
- 1 tsp. cumin seeds
- 1 tsp. turmeric powder
- 2 tsp. red pepper flakes, plus more for garnish
- 1 1/2 cups dried yellow split peas
- 1 lemon, juiced (2 Tbs.)
- 1/2 cup cilantro leaves, for garnish, optional

Directions

1. Set rice cooker setting to "sauté" (or similar), and preheat 2 to 3 minutes. Add coconut oil, and heat 1 minute more. Add onion, garlic, and carrots, and sauté 5 to 6 minutes, or until vegetables are softened. Add cumin, turmeric, and red pepper flakes; cook 1 minute more.
2. Adjust rice cooker setting to "slow cook" (or similar). Pour in 4 cups water, stir in split peas, and season with salt and pepper, if desired. Cover, and cook 3 to 4 hours, or until peas are soft. Thin dal with water, if desired. Serve drizzled with lemon juice, and garnish with cilantro (if using).

Nutritional Information

- Calories: 334
- Fat: 10g
- Carbs: 20g
- Protein: 24g

Chicken & Daikon Soup

Preparation Time: 2 Hours

Yield: 4 Servings

Ingredients

- 500g chicken skin removed & chopped to smaller pieces
- 1 litre of water
- 5 slices of ginger
- 1 daikon (white radish) about 300g, peeled and cut to large chunks
- 8 shiitake mushrooms stems removed
- 1 tbsp wolfberries soaked in water until puffy; drained
- 3 dried scallops
- salt to taste

Directions

1. Add water to the rice cooker pot, set to "Cook". When the water boils, add chicken in the rice cooker for 5-8 minutes with the rice cooker covered and discard the first change of cooking liquid. Set aside blanched chicken pieces.
2. Add 1 litre of water to the rice cooker pot, cover and set to 'Cook'.
3. When the water boils, add chicken, daikon, mushrooms, dried scallops and ginger. Cover the rice cooker and return to a boil. I leave the soup in the 'Cook' mode for about 45 minutes.

4. Switch the rice cooker to 'Warm' and allow to simmer for at least another 1-2 hours. 15 to 30 minutes before serving the soup, add the soaked wolfberries. Add salt to taste.

Nutritional Information

- Calories: 184
- Fat: 3g
- Carbs: 20g
- Protein: 20g

ULTIMATE SHRIMP SOUP

Preparation Time: 20 Minutes

Yield: 4 Servings

Ingredients

- 6 cups Vegetable or Chicken Broth
- 3 cups Button Mushrooms, sliced
- 3 Lemongrass Stalks, about an inch long each
- 3 stalks Galangal Ginger, about an inch long each
- 10 Lime Leaves
- 7 teaspoons Fish Sauce
- 5 Thai Chile Peppers, crushed
- 3 Tomatoes, diced
- 1 Onion, sliced and cut in half
- 1 Lime, juiced
- 2 cups Firm Tofu, cubed
- 6 pieces Whole Prawns
- Cilantro & Green Onions, chopped
- Salt, to taste

Directions

1. Add vegetable or chicken broth into the inner pot and set your rice cooker on steam. Once the broth boils add the lime leaves, galangal and lemongrass and let steep with lid closed for 30 minutes.
2. Add mushrooms, fish sauce, Thai chilli, lime juice, tomatoes, onions and tofu, prawns and cook for another 10-15 minutes. Garnish with cilantro and green onions.

Nutritional Information

- Calories: 184
- Fat: 3g
- Carbs: 20g
- Protein: 20g

TOM YUM SOUP

Preparation Time: 20 Minutes

Yield: 4 Servings

Ingredients

- 100g long grain rice
- 900ml water
- 1 chicken breast, cubed
- 4 slices ginger
- 25g dried scallops (optional)
- 1 1/2 tsp salt, or to taste

To garnish:

- 1 spring onion, sliced
- White pepper

Directions

1. Wash the rice in the rice cooker bowl. Wash and drain the water repeatedly until the water runs clear, this can take about 3-4 times.
2. Prepare the chicken breast, ginger and spring onion.
3. Prepare the dried scallops by immersing them in a bowl of warm water. After 30 seconds break them up with your hands so that you get strips.
4. Add water to the rice in the rice cooker bowl. Then add the chicken, ginger and dried scallops. Close the lid.
5. Cook for 25 minutes. Give it a stir to feel the consistency. It should feel quite runny without too much water left. If it's too runny, leave for another 3 minutes and check. If it's too thick or gets too thick then add water and stir and leave for another 3 minutes so that it heats up again.
6. Add salt, to taste. Garnish with spring onions and a sprinkling of white pepper.

Nutritional Information

- Calories: 181
- Fat: 6g
- Carbs: 21g
- Protein: 12g

CLEAR VEGETABLE BROTH SOUP

Preparation Time: 1 Hour

Yield: 4 Servings

Ingredients

- 3 tomatoes, halved
- 2 carrots, large, chopped into chunks
- 4 sweetcorn cobettes (or 2 sweetcorns)
- 2 potatoes, peeled and sliced
- 5 mushrooms, sliced

- 2 litres water, to fill rice cooker
- 1-2 tsp salt, or to taste

Directions

1. Prepare vegetables.
2. Stick all the vegetables in the rice cooker. Add the water and close the lid.
3. Cook for 1 hour to 1.5 hours.
4. Add 1-2 tsp salt or to taste.

Nutritional Information

- Calories: 181
- Fat: 6g
- Carbs: 21g
- Protein: 12g

HAINANESE CHICKEN RICE

Preparation Time: 20 Minutes

Yield: 4 Servings

Ingredients

- 6 chicken drumsticks, approx 1 1/2 pounds
- 1 dash ground black pepper
- 2 Tbsp sesame oil
- 2 cups rice, uncooked - use the measuring cup that came with your rice cooker!
- 3 cups chicken stock
- 1/2 inch of ginger, cut into thin strips
- 3 cloves garlic, chopped
- 3 pandan leaves, tied into a knot (optional)
- scallions for garnish

- hot sauce, recommended: sriracha or sambal oelek for serving

Directions

1. Rub sesame oil on chicken drumsticks. Top with a pinch of black pepper. Let marinade for about 20 minutes.
2. Wash and drain rice. Put in rice cooker.
3. Add chicken stock, ginger, garlic and pandan leaves (Fill chicken stock to the 2-cup line in your rice cooker).
4. Arrange the chicken drumsticks over the rice.
5. Turn on the rice cooker and let it cook.
6. When rice cooker shuts off, remove the lid and let it sit for about 10 more minutes.
7. Remove the chicken from the rice cooker.
8. Fluff the rice with a fork or a pair of chopsticks.
9. Serve rice with chicken and hot sauce.
10. Garnish with scallions.

Nutritional Information

- Calories: 170
- Fat: 1g
- Carbs: 21g
- Protein: 6g

RICE COOKER MISO SOUP

Preparation Time: 15 Minutes

Yield: 4 Servings

Ingredients

- 4 cups water
- ½ package (10 oz.) soft tofu, cut into ½" cubes
- 1 cup baby spinach

- 2 Tbsp. miso
- 2 scallions, chopped

Directions

1. Add the water to the rice cooker pot, cover, and set to Cook. When the water boils, add the tofu and simmer, covered for 3 minutes. Stir in spinach and simmer for 30 seconds.
2. Ladle about 2 tablespoons soup liquid from the rice cooker into a small bowl. Add the miso to the bowl and stir to dissolve the miso; then stir the contents of the bowl back into the rice cooker pot, set it to Warm, and cover it. Let soup sit for about 5 minutes and garnish with green onions before serving.

Nutritional Information

- Calories: 50
- Fat: 2g
- Carbs: 3g
- Protein: 6g

8. Noodles Recipes

Instant Noodles in Rice Cooker

Preparation Time: 10 Minutes

Yield: 4 Servings

Ingredients

- 1 packet ramen noodles

Directions

1. Fill the pot with water, enough to cover the noodles.
2. Add the dry noodles (break them if necessary).
3. Close the rice cooker's lid.
4. Set the rice cooker to "Cook" mode.
5. Check the noodles after five minutes (rice cookers take longer to boil).
6. Scatter the cooked noodles inside the rice cooker.
7. Add the seasoning that comes with the noodles.
8. Mix the noodles and the seasoning.
9. Add meat and vegetables if you want.
10. Leave the rice cooker on for one more minute to perfectly combine the contents.

Nutritional Information

- Calories: 150
- Fat: 6g
- Carbs: 10g
- Protein: 6g

Noodles and Vegetables

Preparation Time: 20 Minutes

Yield: 4 Servings

Ingredients

- 1 pound of spaghetti
- Vegetables of your choice (zucchini pictured)
- 2 garlic cloves chopped or 1 tsp dried
- 2 tsps fresh parsley or 1 tsp dried
- a pinch of sea salt (to taste)
- 1 jar of tomato sauce of your choice

For the sauce

- 2 tbsp olive oil
- 3 large tomatoes diced or 1 14-oz can diced tomatoes, drained
- 3 cloves of garlic crushed chopped

Directions

1. Pour water into the rice cooker and allow the water to get to a high simmer, very close to a boil
2. Add in pasta and watch closely; boil till al dente (just a tad under done)
3. Pull and drain pasta
4. Vegetables: Chop and steam the veggies separately, with 1 tsp oregano and salt/pepper to taste.
5. Pour olive oil in rice cooker, add in tomatoes and garlic and simmer for 10 min
6. Finally, add pasta and vegetables back into the rice cooker, stir and then serve! If desired, top with a little Parmesan cheese — and enjoy!

Nutritional Information

- Calories: 150
- Fat: 6g
- Carbs: 10g
- Protein: 6g

Easy Chicken Pasta Noodles

Preparation Time: 20 Minutes

Yield: 4 Servings

Ingredients

- 125 g dry pasta, your choice
- 1½ cups water
- 2 tomato, diced
- 1 onion, diced
- ¾ cup tomato puree
- 2 tbsp sugar
- ½ tsp salt
- ¼ cup vegetable oil
- 2 tsps chopped garlic
- 2 tbsps butter
- 1½ cups chicken mince
- Shaved parmesan, to taste
- Fresh basil, to garnish

Directions

1. Place all the ingredients into the inner pan.
2. Mix ingredients thoroughly, and close the outer lid.
3. Press 'Menu Select' key to select 'White Rice' mode, and then press Start key.

4. Wait until you hear the beep sounds indicating that cooking is done.
5. Sprinkle with shaved parmesan and garnish with basil to serve.

Nutritional Information

- Calories: 302
- Fat: 19g
- Carbs: 19g
- Protein: 14g

BRAISED HAKUSAI CHINESE CABBAGE WITH DRIED SCALLOPS & SHIRATAKI

Preparation Time: 20 Minutes

Yield: 4 Servings

Ingredients

- 1/2 large hakusai (chunked)
- 8 pcs dried scallop (soaked)
- 3 pcs garlic (minced)
- 2 tbsp miso paste
- 300ml water
- 1 chicken cube
- 3-4 tbsp wolfberry (soaked)
- 1 packet of shirataki (200g)
- 2 tbspss oil
- 2 tbs sesame oil
- 2 tbsps corn flour
- 1 tbsp sugar
- 2 stalks spring onion (diced)
- 3 chilli pepper (diced)

Directions

1. Place garlic, oil and sesame oil in rice cooker. I'm using the Panasonic Rice Cooker SR-MG182 for this dish.
2. Press "Menu Select" to select "Steam" menu, press "Cooker Timer" to 3 mins.
3. Close the lid then press "Start". Wait until it beeps.
4. Add hakusai, press "Menu Select" to select "Steam" menu then press "Cooking Timer" to 5 mins.
5. Close the lid then press "Start". Wait until it beeps.
6. Stir well then add in the miso paste mixed in water and chicken cube.
7. Press "Menu Select" to select "Steam" menu then press "Cooking Timer" to 15 mins.
8. Close the lid then press "Start". Wait until it beeps.
9. Stir well then add dried scallops and wolfberry, press "Menu Select" to select "Steam" menu then press "Cooking Timer" to 15 mins.
10. Close the lid then press "Start". Wait until it beeps.
11. Stir well then add shirataki, corn flour and sugar, press "Menu Select" to select "Steam" menu then press "Cooking Timer" to 10 mins.
12. Garnish with spring onion and chilli paddi {optional}.
13. Serve hot.

Nutritional Information

- Calories: 150
- Fat: 5g
- Carbs: 10g
- Protein: 6g

RICE COOKER SPAGHETTI WITH MEATBALLS

Preparation Time: 20 Minutes

Yield: 4 Servings

Ingredients

- 26 ounces spaghetti sauce
- 3 1/2 cups water
- 1/2 lb spaghetti
- 1 lb frozen meatballs
- 2 large garlic cloves
- 2 tablespoons dried parsley
- 1 teaspoon dried Italian seasoning

Directions

1. Combine all ingredients in cooking bowl in order listed.
2. Place bowl into rice cooker and plug in the appliance; the warm light will come on.
3. Push the on switch to cook and place the lid on the cooker.
4. Set kitchen timer and cook for 20 minutes.
5. Test pasta for doneness.
6. Place the lid back on the cooker and if necessary, cook several minutes longer until pasta is tender,
7. Serve immediately.

Nutritional Information

- Calories: 302
- Fat: 19g
- Carbs: 19g
- Protein: 14g

CREAMY RICE COOKER MACARONI

Preparation Time: 20 Minutes

Yield: 4 Servings

Ingredients

- 2 cups macaroni

- 1 cup chicken stock or 1 cup water
- 1 cup heavy cream or 1 cup half-and-half
- 1 1/2 cups shredded mixed cheeses (mild cheddar, Vermont cheddar, mozzarella, and fontina)
- 2 tablespoons butter
- 1/2 teaspoon salt and pepper
- 1 pinch cayenne pepper

Directions

1. Place pasta and liquids into rice cooker. Close lid and press cook.
2. When pasta goes to keep warm, add the other ingredients, stir with paddle.
3. Close lid and keep on warm till ready to serve. Stays terrific for hours.
4. If larger serving is desired, go ahead and double or triple recipe. However, when adding the cheese, you may need to add an additional 1/2 cup of liquid if the pasta is not cooked enough, then press cook again.

Nutritional Information

- Calories: 249
- Fat: 12g
- Carbs: 20g
- Protein: 10g

YUM PASTA NOODLES

Preparation Time: 20 Minutes

Yield: 4 Servings

Ingredients

- 1 lb pasta

- 2 1/2 cups water
- 26 ounces marinara sauce
- ground beef (optional) or meatballs (optional) or sausage (optional)

Directions

1. If you have raw meat or sausage you'd like to add, first cook them in the rice cooker pan on Quick Cook or Cook setting.
2. If you have spaghetti or linguine, break it in half and layer the dry pasta in the rice cooker pan with the meat, if there is any. For other types of pasta you won't need to break it to fit it in the pot. Add water and sauce.
3. Turn on rice cooker to cook. Stir frequently. When it shuts down to warm, check the pasta to be sure it's done. If it isn't quite done, add some water, stir and turn on to cook again.
4. For vegetarians omit the ground beef, meatballs and the sausage.

Nutritional Information

- Calories: 249
- Fat: 12g
- Carbs: 20g
- Protein: 10g

RICE NOODLES WITH BEEF

Preparation Time: 20 Minutes

Yield: 4 Servings

Ingredients

- 2 tablespoons vegetable oil
- 1/2 pound ground beef
- 1 clove garlic, peeled and finely minced

- 1 tablespoon black bean paste
- 1/4 pound broccoli florets, blanched
- 2 tablespoons water
- 1/2 pound dried rice stick noodles, soaked in warm water for 10 minutes or until softened
- 1 tablespoon soy sauce
- 2 green onions, thinly sliced, divided

Directions

1. Add the oil to the rice cooker, cover, and set to Cook. When the base of the rice cooker gets warm, add the ground beef and cook for 10 minutes until the beef completely cooks through, covered and stirring occasionally. Leaving the remaining oil in the pot, remove the beef from the pot and set aside.
2. Add the garlic, black bean paste, broccoli and water to the pot and cook for 3 minutes until vegetables are tender.
3. Add the noodles, soy sauce and half the green onions. Mix well.
4. Return the beef to the pot and mix well with the noodles. Garnish with remaining green onions before serving.

Nutritional Information

- Calories: 249
- Fat: 12g
- Carbs: 20g
- Protein: 10g

EASY SPAGHETTI IN A RICE COOKER

Preparation Time: 20 Minutes

Yield: 4 Servings

Ingredients

- Self-timing rice cooker
- 1/2 pound uncooked spaghetti
- 3 cups water
- 1/2 teaspoon salt
- 1/2 teaspoon olive oil
- 1 jar of pasta sauce, if desired

Directions

1. Break the dry spaghetti in half so it will fit in the rice cooker.
2. Pour the water into the cooker, along with the dry spaghetti, and add olive oil and salt.
3. Turn the cooker on and allow the spaghetti to cook for one cycle. You may need to periodically turn the cooker on again as it might turn itself off, since it is calibrated to cook rice, not spaghetti.
4. Check if the spaghetti is al dente, or slightly undercooked, after the cooker turns itself off.
5. Add pasta sauce to the spaghetti in the cooker, and turn the cooker on again. Allow the pasta to cook all the way through. Make sure to stir periodically.

Nutritional Information

- Calories: 221
- Fat: 6g
- Carbs: 20g
- Protein: 10g

RICE COOKER NOODLES WITH MUSHROOMS AND CORN

Preparation Time: 20 Minutes

Yield: 4 Servings

Ingredients

- 1 tsp. oyster sauce
- 1 tsp. dark soy sauce
- ½ tsp. sugar
- 2 cups vegetable stock, divided
- ¼ lb. cellophane (bean thread) noodles
- 1 cup warm water
- 2 Tbsps. vegetable oil
- 2 cloves garlic, finely minced
- 2 cups shiitake mushrooms, diced
- 2 large carrots, peeled and julienned
- ½ cup frozen corn kernels
- ¼ tsp. salt
- ⅛ tsp. ground black pepper

Directions

1. Mix oyster sauce, soy sauce, sugar, and 1 cup stock in a bowl. Set aside. Place noodles in a medium bowl and cover with water. Set aside for 10 minutes, then drain.
2. Add the oil to the rice cooker, cover, and set to Cook. When the base of the rice cooker gets warm, add garlic, mushrooms, carrots, and corn. Fry about 5 minutes until fragrant, covering rice cooker occasionally in the process of frying.
3. Add the oyster sauce mixture, cover the rice cooker, and cook until slightly bubbling, about 5 minutes. Add remaining 1 cup stock, cover the rice cooker, and simmer the mixture for 5 minutes, switching to Warm if mixture bubbles too vigorously.
4. Add noodles, salt, and pepper. Mix well and allow noodles to absorb the sauce mixture.

Nutritional Information

- Calories: 150
- Fat: 6g
- Carbs: 20g
- Protein: 3g

9. Vegetable and Egg Recipes

<u>Vegetable Biryani</u>

Preparation Time: 60 Minutes

Yield: 4 Servings

Ingredients

- 3 Cups Basmati Rice
- 4 potatoes Medium
- 3 carrots Big
- 250 grams French beans
- 1/2 Cup Peas
- 3 Onions
- 6 Green Chillies
- 2 Teaspoons Mixed spices (garam masala)
- 2 Teaspoons Ginger Garlic and paste
- 400gGrams sour curd
- 2 bunches of Mint leaves
- 3 bunches of Coriander leaves
- To taste Salt
- 3 strands Saffron soaked in warm milk
- 1 lime Big
- 2 Tablespoons Ghee (clarified butter)

Directions

1. Clean and cut carrot and beans into 1 inch bits. Steam cook them with peas and salt and set aside. Peel potatoes and cut into wedges. Fry potato wedges and set aside. Wash rice and add 1:2 water and set aside.

2. In a frying pan, add oil and ghee, garam masala, finely sliced onions and green chillies. When golden brown, add ginger garlic paste, beaten curd, vegetables, salt, chopped mint and coriander leaves. Let them cook together and add lime juice.
3. In a rice cooker vessel, place the washed rice with water and add the vegetable curry to it. Let the vegetable biryani cook together. When half done, gently turn the contents, so that the vegetables do not settle on top. Add saffron soaked in milk while turning the biryani.
4. When the rice is ready, serve hot with raita or curd chutney.

Nutritional Information

- Calories: 202
- Fat: 6g
- Carbs: 20g
- Protein: 7g

Vegetable Curry Rice

Preparation Time: 20 Minutes

Yield: 4 Servings

Ingredients

- 1 cup brown rice (I used jasmine brown)
- 1 cup regular coconut milk
- 1.5 to 2 cups water
- ½ teaspoon turmeric
- ¼ teaspoon garlic powder
- ¼ teaspoon onion powder (optional)
- ½ teaspoon salt (more to taste)
- 1 large broccoli crown

- 1 to 2 cups baby carrots
- ¾ can garbanzo beans (chickpeas)
- fresh ground pepper

Directions

1. Put the rice, coconut milk, water, turmeric, onion powder, garlic powder, and salt in the rice cooker and click "on." I used 2 cups of water, but you may need a little less depending on the rice you use.
2. Cut the broccoli into florets, and place the florets and the baby carrots in the steamer basket that goes atop the rice cooker (or steam atop the stove). If using the rice cooker to steam, allow the rice to cook for ten minutes before placing the vegetable steamer atop them.
3. When the rice cooker goes "click." It is all done.
4. Chop the cooked vegetables into bite sized pieces, and toss them into the rice cooker along with the garbanzo beans.
5. Stir to mix all of the ingredients together, add some fresh ground pepper and a touch more salt to taste, and serve!

Nutritional Information

- Calories: 188
- Fat: 10g
- Carbs: 20g
- Protein: 6g

VEGETABLE PILAF

Preparation Time: 30 Minutes

Yield: 4 Servings

Ingredients

- Basmati Rice – 2 cup
- 2 Onions (sliced)

- 2 Carrots (peeled and chopped 1 inch)
- 8 French Beans (chopped 1 inch)
- Green peas – 1/2 cup
- Bay leaf – 2
- Black cardamom – 2
- Cumin seeds – 2 tsps
- Garam masala – 1 tsp
- Few mint leaves
- Salt to taste
- Ghee – 2 tbsps (vegans can use vegetable oil)
- Coriander leaves for garnishing

Directions

1. Clean and soak rice in some water for 20 minutes. Drain the water completely and keep it ready.
2. Add ghee in a frying pan and when ghee is warm, add cumin seeds, black cardamom, bay leaf, sliced onions and saute on low flame.
3. When onions turn translucent, add green peas, carrot, beans and mix well.
4. Add garam masala and mix well. Remove from flame.
5. Firstly add rice in rice cooker with 4 cups of water.
6. Now add the fried vegetables, few mint leaves, salt and mix well.
7. Close the cooker and let it cook till indicator in rice cooker comes to warm.
8. You can stir gently and garnish coriander leaves before serving.

Nutritional Information

- Calories: 190
- Fat: 6g

- Carbs: 20g
- Protein: 11g

RICE COOKER FIESTA MEXICAN RICE

Preparation Time: 20 Minutes

Yield: 4 Servings

Ingredients

- 1 Cup white uncooked rice
- 2 Tbsps. Extra Virgin Olive Oil
- 1 med onion diced
- 2 cloves garlic diced
- 1 Can (about 15 oz) of diced tomatoes (I used fired roasted)
- 1 small can of diced green chilies
- 1 Can of beans (about 15 oz) drained and rinsed (pinto or black beans are perfect)
- 1 Cup chicken broth (use vegetable broth for a vegetarian recipe)
- 1 Cup of corn (I used a leftover ear of grilled corn removed from cob, adds great flavor, but frozen would be fine)
- 2 tsps ground Cumin
- 1 tsp of Smoked Hot Paprika (if you do not have, substitute with cayenne)
- 1/2 tsp dried Oregano

Directions

1. In a frying pan, brown rice in Extra Virgin Olive Oil to make it toasty. This is what adds the nutty flavor to traditional Mexican rice. Add onions and garlic, stirring often until onions are beginning to turn translucent.

2. Lightly spray inner part of rice cooker with cooking spray and add rice/onion mixture. Combine remaining ingredients, set cooker to cook.
3. When cooker turns to warm setting, give a stir and return cover. Let stand for another 10 minutes.
4. Serve with fresh cilantro and sour cream or shredded cheese if desired.

Nutritional Information

- Calories: 190
- Fat: 3g
- Carbs: 20g
- Protein: 11g

PERFECT HARD BOILED EGGS

Preparation Time: 10 Minutes

Yield: 4 Servings

Ingredients

- 5 eggs

Directions

1. Place the steamer rack into the cooker Pot.
2. Add 1 cup of cold water to the cooker Pot.
3. Place the eggs on the steamer rack and use tin foil to hold them in place so they don't move around when cooking.
4. Set cooker Pot (using the manual settings) to cook on high pressure for 6 minutes.
5. Carefully release the steam when done and place eggs immediately in cold running water to cool down. Peel and enjoy.

6. 6 minutes gets the egg yolk to just a tiny bit soft still (see photos). If you prefer them softer or harder, adjust the cook time by 1 minute up or down.

Nutritional Information

- Calories: 77
- Fat: 5g
- Carbs: 1g
- Protein: 6g

RICE COOKER SAAG

Preparation Time: 20 Minutes

Yield: 4 Servings

Ingredients

- 2 tablespoons ghee
- 2 onions, diced
- 4 teaspoons minced garlic
- 2 teaspoons minced ginger

Spices

- 2 teaspoons salt
- 1 teaspoon coriander
- 1 teaspoon ground cumin
- 1 teaspoon garam masala
- ½ teaspoon black pepper
- ½ teaspoon cayenne, adjust to taste
- ½ teaspoon turmeric
- 1 pound spinach, rinsed
- 1 pound mustard leaves, rinsed
- Pinch of kasoori methi (dried fenugreek leaves)

- Ghee or butter, for serving

Directions

1. Press the "saute" button on the cooker Pot and add the ghee. Once it melts, add the onion, garlic, ginger and spices to the pot and stir-fry for 2-3 minutes.
2. Add the spinach, stirring until it wilts and there's enough room to add the mustard greens.
3. Secure the lid, close the pressure valve and cook for 15 minutes at high pressure.
4. Naturally release pressure.
5. Remove the lid and use an immersion blender to puree the contents of the pot (or pour the contents into a blender and then add the blended mixture back into the pot).
6. Stir in the dried fenugreek leaves.
7. Serve with ghee.

Nutritional Information

- Calories: 196
- Fat: 17g
- Carbs: 8g
- Protein: 5g

SAVOY CABBAGE WITH CREAM SAUCE

Preparation Time: 20 Minutes

Yield: 4 Servings

Ingredients

- 1 cup bacon/ lardons, diced
- 1 onion, chopped
- 2 cups bone broth
- 1 medium head Savoy cabbage, chopped finely (about 2lb)

- ¼ tsp mace
- ½ can or 200ml coconut milk (scant 1 cup)
- 1 bay leaf
- Sea salt, to taste
- 2 tbsp parsley flakes

Directions

1. Prepare a parchment round by tracing around the inner pot on a piece of parchment paper and then cutting it out
2. Press 'Saute' and allow the inner pot to heat up
3. Once 'Hot' is displayed, fry the bacon and onions in the inner pot until the bacon is crisp and the onions are lightly browned and translucent
4. Add in the bone broth and scrape the bottom of the pot to remove any stuck browned bits
5. Stir in the cabbage and bay leaf
6. Cover with the parchment round and shut the lid, setting the sealing valve to 'sealing'
7. Select 'Manual' and adjust the cooking time to 4 minutes
8. Once the Pot beeps at the end of the cooking cycle, press 'Keep warm/ cancel' and release the pressure before uncovering and removing the parchment round
9. Press 'Saute', bring to a boil and add in the mace or nutmeg and coconut milk
10. Simmer for 5 minutes, then turn off the Pot and stir in the parsley flakes before serving.

Nutritional Information

- Calories: 63
- Fat: 5g
- Carbs: 3g
- Protein: 1g

Artichokes with Lemon Tarragon Dipping Sauce

Preparation Time: 20 Minutes

Yield: 4 Servings

Ingredients

- 4 artichokes, 5 to 6 ounces each
- 2 small lemons
- 2 cups poultry bone broth
- 1 Tbsp finely chopped tarragon leaves
- 1 stalk celery
- 1/2 cup extra-virgin olive oil
- 1/4 tsp sea salt

Directions

1. Trim the stems of the artichokes so that they are one inch in length. Cut off one inch of the "petals" from the opposite end of the artichokes. Discard the stems and petal tips.
2. Zest the lemons and set aside. Cut four thin slices (about 1/4-inch) from the middle of one zested lemon, removing any seeds.
3. Place the lemon slices in the cooker and top each lemon slice with a trimmed artichoke, stem-side up. Pour in the broth around the artichokes.
4. Close and lock the lid. Press MANUAL for high pressure. Set cooking time to 20 minutes. Once time is up, quick release the pressure.
5. While the artichokes are cooking, make the dipping sauce. Finely chop fresh tarragon leaves. Trim both ends of one stalk of celery and chop into small pieces.

6. Peel the remaining lemon and cut the white pith away with a paring knife. Coarsely chop the fruit. Throw away the seeds.
7. Place the lemon zest, lemon fruit, tarragon, chopped celery, olive oil, and salt in a blender or food processor and blend until thick and creamy.
8. Serve the artichokes with the dipping sauce. Feel free to drink the broth remaining in the cooker.

Nutritional Information

- Calories: 110
- Fat: 5g
- Carbs: 10g
- Protein: 4g

BRUSSELS SPROUTS

Preparation Time: 10 Minutes

Yield: 4 Servings

Ingredients

- 2 tablespoons of coconut oil
- 1/2 cup of onion (yellow, white or even a few shallots would work best), chopped
- 1.5 – 2 teaspoons of minced garlic
- 3 strips of bacon, chopped
- 1 lb of Brussels spouts, outer leaves removed and cleaned (leave whole)
- 1/2 cup water
- Salt and Pepper to Taste
- Butter, optional

Directions

1. Turn your cooker on Sauté
2. Add your coconut oil to the pot
3. Add your chopped onion and minced garlic and sauté for a minute
4. Add in your chopped bacon
5. Sauté until your onions are translucent and bacon crisps up
6. Add your prepared, whole Brussels Sprouts with a 1/2 cup of water
7. Salt and Pepper to Taste
8. Give it a quick stir to incorporate everything
9. Put on your lid, making sure that your vent is closed
10. Set on Manual for 3 minutes on LOW PRESSURE
11. Once cooking is completed (listen for that beep) do a quick release
12. Open your lid when ready and drop in a bit of butter and stir (optional)
13. Drain out the liquid

Nutritional Information

- Calories: 60
- Fat: 1
- Carbs: 12g
- Protein: 5g

GREEN BEANS WITH BACON

Preparation Time: 20 Minutes

Yield: 4 Servings

Ingredients

- 1 cup onion diced
- 5 slices bacon diced
- 6 cups green beans cut in half
- 1 teaspoon salt

- 1 teaspoon pepper
- 1/4 cup water

Directions

1. Turn your cooker on Sauté, and follow the steps in this order.
2. Cut up the bacon and put it in the hot pressure cooker.
3. Start dicing the onion and put it in as you cut it.
4. Stir the bacon and onions and start cutting up the green beans.
5. Add the beans, water, salt and pepper to the pot.
6. Cook on high pressure for 4 minutes, and release all pressure immediately.
7. Taste and add salt and pepper as needed before serving.

Nutritional Information

- Calories: 122
- Fat: 7g
- Carbs: 10g
- Protein: 4g

10. Desserts

Pumpkin Pie Pudding

Preparation Time: 30 Minutes

Yield: 4 Servings

Ingredients

- 2 eggs
- 1/2 cup heavy whipping cream (or almond milk for dairy-free)
- 3/4 cup Erythritol (sub Swerve, Truvia, Splenda or sweetener of choice)
- 15 ounces canned pumpkin puree
- 1 teaspoon pumpkin pie spice
- 1 teaspoon vanilla

For Finishing

- 1/2 cup heavy whipping cream

Directions

1. Whisk together the 2 eggs and add all remaining ingredients in the order listed.
2. Grease a 6-inch x 3-inch pan very, very well. I found this easiest to do with a silicone basting brush so I could get into all the nooks and crannies.
3. Pour the mixture into the pan.
4. In the inner liner of your cooker, place 1.5 cups of water.
5. Place a steamer rack on top of it and place the pan with the pumpkin mixture on the rack.
6. Cover the pan with a silicone lid or aluminum foil.

7. Cook for 20 minutes at high pressure, and allow it to release pressure naturally for 10 minutes. Release all remaining pressure.
8. Remove lid carefully, not allowing any of the water on the lid to fall back into the pudding.
9. Chill for 6-8 hours and serve with additional whipped cream.

Nutritional Information

- Calories: 184
- Fat: 16g
- Carbs: 8g
- Protein: 3g

MOLTEN BROWNIE CUPS

Preparation Time: 20 Minutes

Yield: 4 Servings

Ingredients

- ⅔ cup sugar-free chocolate chips or paleo friendly chips
- 6 tbsp salted butter
- 3 eggs
- ⅔ cup Swerve granular sweetener
- 3 ½ tbsp almond flour
- 1 tsp vanilla extract

Directions

1. Spray four 6-ounce ramekins with non-stick coconut oil spray and set
2. On the stovetop in a small saucepan over medium-low heat, add sugar-free chocolate chips and butter. Stir and

heat until melted and blended. Remove from heat and set aside.
3. In a large bowl combine: eggs, Swerve sweetener, almond flour, and vanilla extract. Whisk to mix thoroughly.
4. Pour the melted chocolate mixture into the egg and flour mixture and whisk to combine thoroughly.
5. Fill each ramekin halfway full with the brownie batter.
6. Add 1 ¾ cup water to the inner pot of the Pot and place the steamer rack (trivet) into the inner pot.
7. Place three of the ramekins on top of the rack and stack the other ramekin in the center and on top of the three bottom ramekins.
8. Close and lock the lid. Flip the pressure release handle to the Sealing position. Select the Pressure Cook (Manual) on High-Pressure setting and use the + or - buttons to set the cooking time for 9 minutes.
9. Once the cooking time is complete, carefully (using oven mitts or a wooden spoon to flip the steam release handle to Venting and keeping face & hands away from steam) use the Quick release method to release all the pressure.
10. Once the all the steam has released and pin drops, open the lid and Carefully using oven mitts remove the ramekins from the pot.
11. Let cakes cool for 5 to 7 minutes, and serve warm. Garnish with sugar-free whipped cream if desired.

Nutritional Information

- Calories: 425
- Fat: 36g
- Carbs: 11g
- Protein: 9g

KETO GLUTEN-FREE COCONUT ALMOND CAKE

Preparation Time: 40 Minutes

Yield: 4 Servings

Ingredients

- 1 cup almond flour
- 1/2 cup unsweetened shredded coconut
- 1/3 cup Truvia
- 1 teaspoon baking powder
- 1 teaspoon apple pie spice

Wet ingredients

- 2 eggs lightly whisked
- 1/4 cup butter melted
- 1/2 cup heavy whipping cream

Directions

1. Mix together all the dry ingredients.
2. Pour in wet ingredients one by one, mixing well with each addition.
3. Pour into a 6-inch round cake pan and cover the pan with foil.
4. Place 2 cups of water into your cooker liner, and put in a steamer rack on top.
5. Set your cooker for 40 minutes at High Pressure, let it release pressure naturally for 10 minutes, and release remaining pressure.
6. Carefully take out and pan and let it cool for 15-20 minutes. Upend the cake onto a plate. sprinkle with coconuts, almonds, or powdered sweetener if desired and serve.

Nutritional Information

- Calories: 236
- Fat: 23g
- Carbs: 5g

- Protein: 5g

KETO CARROT CAKE

Preparation Time: 50 Minutes

Yield: 4 Servings

Ingredients

- 3 eggs
- 1 cup almond flour
- 2/3 cup Swerve
- 1 teaspoon baking powder
- 1.5 teaspoons apple pie spice
- 1/4 cup coconut oil
- 1/2 cup heavy whipping cream
- 1 cup carrots shredded
- 1/2 cup walnuts chopped

Directions

1. Grease a 6-inch cake pan.
2. Mix together all ingredients using a hand mixer, until the mixture is well-incorporated, and looks fluffy. This will keep the cake from being dense as almond flour cakes can sometimes be.
3. Pour into the greased pan and cover the pan with foil.
4. In the inner liner of your cooker Pot, place two cups of water, and a steamer rack. Place the foil-covered cake on the trivet.
5. Press the CAKE button and allow it to cook for 40 minutes. Allow the pressure to release naturally for 10 minutes. Release remaining pressure. If you don't have a cake button, just set your pressure cooker for 40 minutes at high pressure.

6. Let it cool before icing with a frosting of your choice or serve plain.

Nutritional Information

- Calories: 268
- Fat: 25g
- Carbs: 6g
- Protein: 6g

CHEESECAKE

Preparation Time: 50 Minutes

Yield: 4 Servings

Ingredients

- 16 oz Cream Cheese room temperature
- 1/2 cup + 2 Tbsp Granulated Swerve
- 1/2 tsp Vanilla Extract
- 1 tsp Fresh Orange Zest dried zest results in a chunky texture
- Zest of 1 Small Lemon
- 3 Eggs room temperature
- 1/4 cup Heavy Whipping Cream

Top Layer

- 1/2 cup Sour Cream or Greek Yogurt full-fat
- 2 tsp Granulated Swerve

Directions

1. Using a 6" (or 7" maximum) push pan or springform pan, take a strip of parchment paper slightly taller than the sides of the pan (a pan with a height of at least 2.5" is best) and line all the way around the perimeter of the pan. Very

lightly oil the bottom of the pan. Wrap a piece of foil around the bottom of the pan. Since we're not using a crust, this will help insure that no water gets into the cheesecake and no cheesecake seeps out of the pan. Set aside.
2. Using a stand mixer or hand-held mixer, blend together cream cheese, Swerve, heavy cream, lemon and orange peels, and vanilla until smooth.
3. Add eggs, one at a time, very gently mixing until just combined. Do not over mix the eggs, otherwise you're cheesecake will be lumpy, not creamy.
4. Pour the filling into the prepared pan. Lay a paper towel on top of the pan and gently wrap a piece of tin foil over the top to hold the foil in place. This is why the parchment needs to be taller than the pan. Set aside.
5. Pour 1-1/2 cups of water into the inner liner pot of the Cooker (use 2 cups for the 8qt models). Place the trivet in the water with the handles up.
6. Take a long piece of tinfoil and fold it in thirds, creating a sling. Place the cheesecake on the center of the foil sling and very gently lift it up using the long piece of foil. Place it into the cooker on the trivet. Leave the sling in the pot.
7. Put the lid on the cooker and set the valve to "Sealing". Press the "Manual" button and increase the time to 37 minutes.
8. While the cheesecake is cooking, prepare the topping. Mix the "Topping" ingredients and set aside.
9. When the cycle ends, let the cooker naturally release pressure (DO NOT open the valve and do a Quick Pressure Release) for 18 minutes. Open the valve and remove the lid when all pressure is released.
10. Carefully lift the cheesecake out of the cooker with the foil sling. Remove the foil and paper towel from the top. If any liquid has accumulated on top of the cheesecake, very gently dab it off with a paper towel.

11. While the cheesecake is still hot (and it's okay if there's a slight jiggle to it in the middle), spread the topping over it.
12. Replace the paper towel/foil lid on the cheesecake and refrigerate for 8 hours or overnight.
13. When completely cooled, release the outer spring ring of the pan or, if using a push pan, push the bottom up out of the pan and remove the out layer of parchment. Cut into 8 slices and serve chilled.

Nutritional Information

- Calories: 268
- Fat: 24g
- Carbs: 3g
- Protein: 7g

KETO CREME BRULEE

Preparation Time: 10 Minutes

Yield: 4 Servings

Ingredients

- 2 cups heavy whipping cream
- 6 large egg yolks
- 5 tablespoons Keto sweetener Use 3 tablespoons for the cream mixture and reserve 2 for the topping
- 1 tablespoon vanilla extract

Directions

1. In a mixing bowl combine heavy whipping cream, yolks, 3 tablespoons sweetener and vanilla.
2. Whisk together until well combined
3. Pour mixture into 6 small ramekins
4. Cover each ramekin individually with aluminum foil
5. Add one cup of water to the bottom of the inner pot

6. Place silicon steamer on top
7. Carefully place three ramekins into the steamer
8. Place the remaining three ramekins on top of the bottom three slightly offsetting them so that the bottom ones will support the top ones.
9. Close lid and make sure valve is set to seal
10. Cook on high pressure for 9 minutes.
11. Let rest for 15 minutes
12. Release steam and open lid
13. Let cool and refrigerate for at least a few hours it's best served cold, but I have been known to eat a warm one right out of the pot. They have more of a custard texture when eaten warm.)
14. Sprinkle 1 teaspoon of Keto sweetener on top of each creme brûlée
15. Place the ramekins onto a cookie sheet, so that you don't end up burning your table or countertop. (Guess how I know that one!)
16. Using a hand torch, burn the sugar until it darkens. Make sure to do this in a well ventilated area and be careful as you are working with an open flame. Just a note, the Keto sweetener will not get the hard crackle of sugar but it does come close, so if you have some non Keto diners, I usually top theirs with real sugar.)

Nutritional Information

- Calories: 337
- Fat: 24g
- Carbs: 3g
- Protein: 7g

THE ULTIMATE RICE COOKER CAKE

Preparation Time: 10 Minutes

Yield: 4 Servings

Ingredients

- 2 cups (300g) self-raising flour
- 2 tbsps white sugar
- 2 eggs, lightly beaten
- 1 1/2 cups (375ml) milk

Directions

1. Place flour, sugar and eggs into a bowl and whisk together while adding milk at a little at a time until all ingredients are incorporated.
2. Pour cake mixture into the bowl of a rice cooker and set the rice cooker to cook. If you have an automatic rice cooker, you may need to push the button down 2-3 times until your cake is cooked.
3. Cook until a skewer inserted into the cake comes out clean or the cake has a smooth, dry surface. This should take around 20-25 minutes.
4. Slice and serve with berries and ice cream or maple syrup.

Nutritional Information

- Calories: 337
- Fat: 24g
- Carbs: 3g
- Protein: 7g

APPLE RICE COOKER CAKE

Preparation Time: 20 Minutes

Yield: 4 Servings

Ingredients

- 200g hotcake mix
- 1/5 sweet potato
- 150mls milk
- 1 egg
- 4 tbsps oil
- 4 tbsps sugar
- 1 apple
- 1/2 Cup butter

Directions

1. Peel, core and slice the apple. Cook with butter in a saucepan.
2. Cut the sweet potato into small-sized cubes and soak in water for 5-10 minutes.
3. In a bowl, mix the hotcake mix, milk, egg, oil and sugar. Add the sweet potato to the bowl and mix.
4. Layer the bottom of the rice cooker with the cooked slices of apples.
5. Pour the batter into the buttered cooker bowl on top of the apple slices and switch the cooker on to a regular white rice setting.
6. Take rice cooker out of machine when the cake is finished cooking and allow the cake to cool in the bowl before removing. Enjoy with cream, custard or a scoop of ice cream.

Nutritional Information

- Calories: 237
- Fat: 22g
- Carbs: 3g
- Protein: 7g

Rice Cooker Upside-Down Pineapple Cake

Preparation Time: 60 Minutes

Yield: 4 Servings

- **Ingredients**
- ¾ cup granulated sugar (150 g)
- 3 oz cream cheese, room temperature (85 g)
- 2 large eggs
- 2 tablespoons pineapple juice, from can
- 5 tablespoons unsalted butter, melted
- 1 cup pancake mix (125 g)
- 7 canned pineapple slices
- 7 maraschino cherries

CARAMEL SAUCE

- ½ cup unsalted butter (115 g)
- 1 cup brown sugar, packed (220 g)
- vanilla ice cream, for serving (optional)

Directions

1. In a large bowl, use a spatula to mix the sugar and cream cheese until well-combined. Whisk in the eggs until there are no lumps remaining.
2. Stir in the pineapple juice, melted butter, and pancake mix until the batter is thick and smooth.
3. Make the caramel sauce: in a small saucepan over medium-high heat, melt the butter, then add the brown sugar. Stir rapidly for 2 to 3 minutes. Remove from the heat once mixture starts to boil and thicken.
4. Pour the caramel sauce into the bottom of a 1-liter rice cooker bowl insert.

5. Place one pineapple slice in the middle of the rice cooker bowl, then arrange the other slices in a ring around it. Place one maraschino cherry in the center of each pineapple slice.
6. Pour the cake batter over the pineapple slices and shake to smooth out the top of the batter.
7. Cook for 60 minutes.
8. Remove the bowl insert from the rice cooker and invert the cake onto a plate.
9. Slice and serve, topped with vanilla ice cream if desired.
10. Enjoy!

Nutritional Information

- Calories: 337
- Fat: 24g
- Carbs: 3g
- Protein: 7g

RICE COOKER LEMON CAKE

Preparation Time: 10 Minutes

Yield: 4 Servings

Ingredients

Cake:

- 3 cups flour
- 1/2 tsp baking soda
- 1/2 tsp salt
- 3/4 cup butter
- 1 cups sugar
- 3 eggs
- 1 cup milk
- 2 tablespoons grated lemon zest

- 2 tablespoons lemon juice

Syrup:

- 1/3 cup water
- 1/3 cup sugar
- 2 tablespoons lemon juice

Glaze:

- 1 cup powdered sugar
- 2 tablespoons lemon juice
- 1 tsp melted butter

Directions

1. Combine dry ingredients, add wet ingredients, cook in the rice cooker on "cake" setting.
2. Brush on syrup while still hot. Drizzle glaze after cooled.

Nutritional Information

- Calories: 217
- Fat: 18g
- Carbs: 3g
- Protein: 5g

Conclusion

I hope you enjoyed all of the delicious "Rice Cooker Recipes" in this cookbook!

Using the rice cooker is fairly simple and for a successful meal, you only need quality ingredients as well as some of your time. The entire cooking process is easy and this type of food preparation does not require constant watching over food that is being cooked.

Printed in Great Britain
by Amazon

87283372R00081